Praise God in Song

ECUMENICAL DAILY PRAYER

Praise God in Song

Compiled and Edited by
JOHN ALLYN MELLOH, SM, and WILLIAM G. STOREY

With original music by
DAVID CLARK ISELE, HOWARD HUGHES, SM, and
MICHAEL JONCAS

Published by
G.I.A. PUBLICATIONS, INC., Chicago, Illinois
G-2270

To the
myrrh-bearing
women

Preface

Throughout the centuries Christians have gathered for communal prayer to give praise to the Lord of history. Daily prayer, morning and evening, enjoys a lengthy tradition and communal prayer forms, employing the perennial elements of hymnody, psalmody, Scripture selections and intercessory prayer, have been one of the mainstays of Christian worship.

In the United States, many major Christian churches have explored this tradition and, during the recent decades of liturgical renaissance, have published official forms for common daily prayer. This book of ecumenical prayer offers a collection of services for morning and evening, arranged simply, so that the riches of this tradition are available in a single volume.

Praise God in Song was born of the experience of daily prayer in varying communities—parochial, university, lay and religious,—and is intended to serve similarly diverse groups. It is designed to provide common prayer forms for gatherings of Christians from different confessions as well as for congregations belonging to the major Christian churches. The standard forms of Morning and Evening Prayer are suitable for parish worship and ecumenical prayer in larger groups; the shorter services for morning and evening and the Resurrection Vigil for Saturday night are appropriate for family prayer and worship in smaller groups.

All the services are presented in full musical setting, commissioned especially for this book. They represent various musical styles, each setting being internally consistent. An exception to this is the plainchant Lord's Prayer used throughout. In addition to the new compositions, supplementary material has been compiled from well-known, contemporary sources. Where an entire setting is the work of a single composer, his name appears only at the beginning of the service. In the settings which include the works of several composers and in the supplements, credits have been given for each piece of music. All of the music contained in this book has been used successfully by different groups praying Morning and Evening Prayer and has been found to support the spirit of prayer.

Grateful acknowledgement is given to the following people who directly assisted in the preparation of this book: to Kathleen Hughes, R.S.C.J. and Rev. John D. Grabner, who helped evaluate and revise materials; to Andrew Ciferni, O. Praem., who contributed the initial texts for the seasonal thanksgivings and also helped with the evaluation and revision of materials; to Barbara Schmich, who did the final editing as well as the design and illustration of the book.

Grateful acknowledgement is also given to the Notre Dame Center for Pastoral Liturgy, University of Notre Dame, for sponsoring the project and for making available their staff and resources, and, finally, to G.I.A. Publications, especially Edward J. Harris and Robert J. Batistini, for their expert assistance and constant support.

John Allyn Melloh, S.M.
William G. Storey

Table of Contents

SUPPLEMENT TABLE

Morning Supplement

Evening Supplement

Vigil Supplement

Introduction

Early Christian Prayer

Under the leadership of James the Just, "the brother of the Lord" (Gal. 1:19), the primitive Judeo-Christian Church at Jerusalem did not break with the normal Judaic patterns of worship and piety.[1] Those Jews who put their faith in Jesus of Nazareth as Yahweh's Anointed continued to be "regular in their visits to the Temple, praising and blessing God" (Lk. 24:53), were daily participants in "the Prayers" (Acts 2:42, 46), "met with one accord in Solomon's portico" (Acts 5:13) and "everyday preached the Good News about Jesus, the Messiah, in the Temple and from house to house" (Acts 5:42). Although as a special fellowship (ḥaburah) of believers in Jesus as Messiah and Lord, they added "the breaking of bread" (Acts 2:46) on the Lord's day to their standard Jewish pieties, they did not abandon such normative practices as the mandatory hours of prayer at dawn and sunset each day. Since both in Palestine and in the Diaspora, Judeo-Christians continued to be members of the local synagogues during the most formative decades of the Church's existence, a synagogal pattern of prayer imposed itself on the early Christian communities.[2]

Moreover, the Lord Jesus himself has participated regularly in Temple (Lk. 2:41; Jn. 2:13; 5:1; 7:2-3, 14; 10:22-24; 12:1, 12) and synagogue worship (Mk. 1:21-22; 6:12; Lk. 4:15-16) and had both practiced (Mt. 14:23; Lk. 6:12; Mk. 1:35) and recommended (Mt. 6:6; Lk. 18:1; Lk. 22:40) constant prayer to his disciples. Apparently he even taught them a model prayer at their request. "You should pray like this: 'Our Father in heaven . . .' " (Mt. 6:9f; Lk. 11:1f).

As a result of their Jewish matrix and the teaching and example of the Lord, the widely-separated churches were at one in diligently fulfilling the apostolic admonition to assembly frequently (Heb. 10:25) and to pray always (I Thess. 5:17; Eph. 6:18; Col. 4:2), everywhere (I Tim. 2:8) and for all (I Tim. 2:1-2). The delay of the Parousia only added special poignancy to their vigilance in prayer. "Stay awake, because you do not know when the master of the house is coming, evening, midnight, cockcrow, dawn; if he comes unexpectedly, he must not find you asleep. And what I say to you I say to all: Stay awake!" (Mk. 12:35-37). To keep up its hope as it awaited "the glorious advent of its great God and Savior Jesus Christ" (Tt. 2:13), the Church was careful to proclaim in Eucharistic word and sign "the Lord's death until he

10

comes" (I Cor. 11:26). Just as it was scrupulous in celebrating the Lord's Supper on the Lord's Day each week, so too it apparently cared deeply about its daily services, the direct legacy of the synagogue and of dominical practice and precept.

Morning and Evening Prayer

If ever there were an apostolic tradition normative for Christian life, it would be the well-established custom of morning and evening prayer. The materials of such prayer derived to some degree from synagogue usages, too. Although trinitarian formulae soon replaced the Shemah[3] and Christians prayed in and through "Christ our Lord," the use of appropriate psalms, canticles, lessons, responses, and intercessory prayers continued, even when supplemented by new Christian compositions, such as the Christological hymns and the doxologies observable in Paul and the Book of Revelation (Eph. 5:14; I Tim. 1:17; 3:16-17; 6:15; Rev. 1:5-6; 4:8; 5:9-10, 12-14).[4]

Sufficient references survive from the pre-Constantinian era to indicate that the "spiritual oblation . . . of psalms and hymns, a sacrifice of prayer" morning and evening, was a generally established fact of Church life.[5] Although the Fathers insisted that the whole life of a true Christian should be one continuous prayer, they did not scorn assigned times of prayer as devotional means toward "unceasing prayer" (Luke 18:1; I Thess. 5:17).[6] It seems highly plausible that the morning and evening observances (the *orationes legitimae* of Tertullian,[7] the *horae antiquitus observatae* of Cyprian[8]) were public, communal hours of prayer. Like pious Jews the early Christians everywhere would have celebrated the customary devotions at dawn and at sunset in common—as churches—whenever they were able to do so. At the very least, one can say that morning and evening were the normative *times* of prayer.

For Rome at the beginning of the third century, the *Apostolic Tradition* of St. Hippolytus provides us with solid evidence for both regular morning and occasional evening assemblies.[9] Although sometimes there would be no morning gathering for prayer and instruction, Hippolytus clearly considers a morning liturgical assembly to be normative and "the place where the Spirit flourishes."[10] Moreover, although his chapter on the communal church-supper *(agape)* has become garbled in transmission, it appears that early Roman Vespers took the form of a non-Eucharistic meal. In the context of a fraternal and charitable dinner presided over by the bishop, the community prayed, sang and engaged in directed conversation. Besides the meal itself one can clearly discern an initial lamp-lighting *(lucernarium)* and thanksgiving *(eucharistia lucernaris)* and the singing of responsorial psalms with hallelujah refrains.[11]

Like other representative third-century Fathers, Hippolytus also knew and recommended other prayer times scattered throughout the day and night.[12] In particular, from the earliest times the Roman Church had attached special importance to the private observance of Terce, Sext and None as hours of our Lord's passion.[13] Nevertheless, even with the multiplication of other prayer moments, the "mandatory, oblgatory, regular, canonical" hours *(orationes legitimae ingressu lucis ac noctis)* remained cardinal and were to have the greatest future. It was clearly Matins and Vespers (Morning and Evening Prayer) that were the most significant, solemn and accessible daily services, and they became the key constituents of the cathedral (parochial) rites after Constantine.[14] Except perhaps for North Africa, daily Mass was abnormal.[15] It was the Liturgy of the Hours that sanctified the day and prolonged the celebration of the Paschal Mystery.

Matins was a daily commemoration of the resurrection of Christ. "We must pray in the morning that the Lord's resurrection may be celebrated by Morning Prayer," as St. Cyprian of Carthage put it.[16] Or as the fourth-century *Testamentum Domini* phrased it: "At dawn we praise God in psalms because Christ praised his Father in company with his apostles after he rose from the dead."[17] Matins invited Christians in union with their risen Lord to walk in newness of life by dedicating their new day to him who "makes all things new" (Rev. 21:5).[18]

The early morning assembly *(coetus antelucani)* of new commitment had an evening assembly at its counterpart *(coetus vespertinus).* Although eventually the old *agape* fell out of common use, the lucernarium, psalmody and intercessory prayer continued and developed. Vespers was thought of in many ways. In some churches it commemorated the Lord's evening sacrifice, his burial and descent among the dead, and his evening institution of the Eucharistic Sacrifice.[19] On the other hand, since evening was considered "the beginning of the following day," Evensong could be interpreted as foreshadowing the Parousia and the final resurrection of the body.[20] Of course, Vespers could also be understood as anticipating natural sleep and the sleep of death, and Christians were expected to use the evening service to render thanks for all the blessings of the past day and for the coming gift of sleep,[21] to repent of what they had done amiss or left undone[22] and to intercede for the needs of the Church and the world:[23] thanksgiving, repentance, petition. Variable psalmody[24] and lessons[25] often extended this basic format.

Vigil of the Resurrection

In addition to Matins and Vespers a typical cathedral Office came to include a *weekly* Vigil of the Resurrection (Vigil of the Myrrh-Bearing Women). Modern research has shown that our ancestors in the faith held a kind of brief Easter Vigil every Saturday night as a concrete way of celebrating the Paschal Mystery.[26] Sometime after the mid-fourth century, Bishop Cyril of Jerusalem (351-386) composed a Vigil of the Resurrection to be conducted at the empty tomb during the night of Saturday to Sunday each week. Naturally it attracted not only the normal members of his own community but also that never ending stream of visitors who came on pilgrimage to "the mother and mistress of all churches." Apparently they enjoyed this special kind of service, wrote home about it and enthusiastically recommended it to their local bishops. Late in Cyril's episcopate, around 381-384, one such pilgrim, a Spanish nun called Egeria, visited Jerusalem and left us a helpful description of the weekly Vigil of the Resurrection. Shortly after midnight on Sunday morning the people begin gathering in large numbers in the courtyard before the tomb "as if it were Easter" and wait in prayer for the liturgical service to begin. The tomb area itself is ablaze with lights awaiting the arrival of the bishop at cockcrow. Around 2 A.M. the bishop enters and goes into the cave-tomb; the Vigil begins with the singing of three responsorial psalms continues with a litany of intercession and climaxes with the bishop proclaiming a gospel of the resurrection at the door of the tomb. The early service then concludes with a brief visit to Calvary.

The success of the Vigil at Jerusalem prompted bishop after bishop of the wider church to institute similar brief weekly Vigils whose chief feature was the singing of a pericope of the resurrection. As a result, the classic cathedral Office came to be composed of daily morning and evening prayer and a weekly vigil. Even when overlaid by later monastic accretions, the earlier popular vigil "Of the Myrrh-Bearing Women" can still be discerned in the early morning services of the Eastern Churches. Of late the *Office of Taizé,* the Roman *Liturgy of the Hours* and the *Lutheran Book of Worship* have all initiated fresh attempts at emphasizing the Sunday by something of the same sort.

A Common Daily Prayer

Thus the present form of daily prayer takes as its model and inspiration the cathedral usages of the patristic church in its prime. Recent historical studies by such distinguished liturgical scholars as Juan Mateos, S.J.,[27] Robert Taft, S.J.,[28] and Professor Gabrielle Winkler[29] have stripped away the accretions of centuries from these original rites and allow us now to recover the solid core of the patristic tradition of corporate worship. Above all, thanks to these studies we can distinguish between the characteristics of parochial and monastic Offices and relearn the appropriate values of both forms of prayer.

This daily Office is also designed as an organic reform growing out of fully ecumenical principles of worship and adapted, especially as regards its music, to modern needs. It stresses a healthy alternation of

13

song and silence, ritual and simplicity, standard format and changeable elements. Although for sound reasons the East Christian tradition has contributed much to its basic shape, this Office does not purport to reproduce any one set of liturgical structures, Eastern or Western, Protestant or Catholic. Rather, it attempts, with fidelity to a well-documented and universal tradition, to arrange a viable form of common daily prayer for our era.

CELEBRATING THE DAILY OFFICE

Order of Service

The order of service is uniform throughout and each service is intended to be used in the order given. Elements of each service follow in the proper sequence, thus eliminating the necessity of excessive page-changing. An exception to this occurs only when alternate material is chosen for use.

It is recommended that initially the services be used without alteration, so that the group may become familiar with the structure of the services and with their rhythm and flow. The use of supplementary material—alternate hymns, psalms, canticles, longer readings, etc.— may profitably be employed when the group has achieved a measure of comfort with the services.

Alternate material may be found in the supplements at the end of each section of the book, arranged in the same order as the services. Additional alternatives may be found through the Appendix. Since an effort has been made to provide musical settings which are stylistically compatible, selections from the supplements or from other sources should be chosen with an eye to this compatibility.

The musical settings may be sung in unison or in four-part harmony; accompaniment with organ or guitar is optional. A trained choir may provide harmonizations for the unison melodies.

For daily prayer, simplicity of form and musical style is the suggested norm; on feast days and during major church seasons, musical and textual elaboration and variety is recommended, though by no means required.

Ministries

Morning and Evening Prayer are, by nature, ecclesial acts and therefore, normatively, expect the presence of an ordained clergy who take the assigned roles of Leader (bishop/presbyter/pastor) and Assistant (deacon/deaconess). In practice, however, most Christian groups gather for daily prayer without benefit of clergy. In such instances, it is understood that "Leader" means any person, lay or religious, male or female, who conducts the service, and "Assistant" indicates a secondary minister who functions in place of an ordained deacon/deaconess. A Cantor is a person skilled in music leadership and a Reader (Lector) is a person trained to proclaim God's word effectively.

The Leader presides over the entire service, prays all the prayers in the name of the community, initiates the Lord's Prayer and gives the Blessing. In the absence of an Assistant, the Leader also sings the Light Proclamation and the Evening Thanksgiving. In this case, the Cantor sings the Litany.

Environment

Since Morning and Evening Prayer are not, normatively, word liturgies or preaching services, but liturgies of praise and prayer, they are not built up around the word as proclaimed/preached. They require, therefore, a different kind of worship space than is usually provided for other services. An auditorium or classroom-like space is unsuitable for the Office and will inevitably militate against this form of prayer whenever it is employed. Consequently, one must try to arrange a space that meets the needs of this particular kind of worship: non-preaching, non-Eucharistic.

Traditionally, this space has been a "choir" and to celebrate in choir meant not only a particular style of celebration proper to the daily Office but also a particular kind of locale. Such choirs for Office still survive in many places and are completely distinct from other kinds of worship space. In form, a choir is a hollow square or rectangle with an apse occupying its east side, the ministers the west side and the congregation the north and south sides.

Although, even outside the time of Eucharist, the Lord's Table remains the chief liturgical appointment, symbolizing the welcoming Lord in our midst, (and therefore is appropriately reverenced upon entering or leaving the church and during the climactic Gospel canticles,) it is clearly not the focus of attention during the Office as it is during the Eucharist. One would not normally, then, highlight the altar space during the hours but carry out the Office in the midst of the assembly: the assistant ministers (deacon, cantor, lector) function *in medio* and the accessories of worship (lectern, candelabrum, brazier/censer) also stand *in medio*. The congregation is split roughly in two halves and each half faces the other. Such an arrangement is altogether preferable to that of an auditorium or lecture hall where everyone faces forward. With this arrangement the ministers of worship clearly lead the prayer but, being in the midst of the other worshipers, are not seen to dominate it. In such an atmosphere, prayer may be experienced as more cordial and communal. The same holds true for smaller gatherings in a common room or dining room where the ambience is essentially more familial and informal.

Vesture

In larger, more formal settings, the ministers would normally wear some type of liturgical vesture: alb, surplice, choir robe. Ordained clergy would also wear the stole appropriate to their rank. In smaller, more informal settings, no special vestures need be worn.

Footnotes

[1]Kenneth L. Caroll, "The Place of James in the Early Church," *Bulletin of the John Rylands Library* 44 (1961-62) 49-67. For the decisive role of Judeo-Christianity before and after 70 A.D., consult Jean Daniélou, *The Theology of Jewish Christianity* (Chicago, 1964) and his *The First Six Hundred Years* (New York, 1964), chaps. 1 and 6.

[2]C. W. Dugmore, *The Influence of the Synagogue on the Divine Office* (London, 1944), chaps. 1-2; Kurt Hruby, "Les Heures de prière dans le judaisme à l'epoque de Jésus," *La Prière des Heures,* ed. Msgr. Cassien and Bernard Botte (Paris, 1963) chap. 3, pp. 59-84; Eric Werner, "The Jewish Liturgy of the Time of Primitive Christianity," *The Sacred Bridge* (New York, 1959), chap. 1, pp. 1-16.

[3]Dugmore, *Influence,* 102-104.

[4]See also the early second-century Christian psalter, the so-called *Odes of Solomon,* each fitted out with an alleluia refrain intended for liturgical use: Johannes Quasten, *Patrology,* I (Westminster, Md., 1962), pp. 160-168.

[5]"There can be no doubt that public worship at dawn and at sunset was the primitive tradition of the early Church:" Dugmore, *Influence,* 112; cf. also p. 57: "Our conclusion is that from the very beginning daily services modelled on the ritual of the Synagogue were common both in the East and in the West." Early Patristic Testimony: Tertullian, *De oratione,* 25, ed. Ernest Evans (London, 1953), p. 34; Hippolytus, *The Apostolic Tradition,* 41, ed. Bernard Botte (LQF, 39; Munster Westfalen, 1963) pp. 88-97; Origen, *On Prayer,* 12, trans. Eric G. Jay (London, 1954), pp. 114-115; Cyprian, *On the Lord's Prayer,* 34-36, trans. Roy J. Deferrari *(Fathers of the Church,* 36; Washington, D.C., 1958), pp. 157-159.

[6]"If some assign definite hours for prayer...yet the Gnostic [the true Christian] prays throughout his whole life." Clement of Alexandria, *Stromata* VII, 7, trans. Eric G. Jay, *Origen's Treatise on Prayer* (London, 1954), p. 37; Hippolytus, *Apostolic Tradition,* chap. 41, ed. Botte, pp. 96-97, thinks of the seven hours of prayer as helps "to keep Christ always before your minds." Tertullian, *De oratione,* 24, ed. Evans, p. 35: "Concerning the times of prayer no rules at all have been laid down, except of course to pray at every time and place... [Nevertheless] we shall not find superfluous the observance of certain hours...;" Cyprian, *On the Lord's Prayer,* 34-36, speaks of Christians as those "who are destined to pray always and to give thanks to God" and yet as having "established and lawful times for prayer."

[7]*De oratione,* 25, p. 35.

[8]*The Lord's Prayer,* 35, p. 157.

[9]Chaps. 25, 35 and 41, pp. 64, 82, 88.

[10]"Ire ad ecclesiam, ubi floret spiritus" (p. 82), "Locus ubi docetur," where a *doctor* gives instruction under the guidance of the Holy Spirit (p. 88). At Alexandria in the same period Origen held daily conferences in Sacred Scripture: *Hom. in Gen.* 10, 3 (PG 12, 218) and *Hom. in Exod.* 7, 8 (PG 12, 349); cf. Daniélou, *First Six Hundred Years,* pp. 164-165.

[11]Responsorial psalmody was especially commended by Tertullian *(De Oratione,* 27, p. 36) and the chief features of Hippolytus' *agape* are corroborated in his *Apology,* 39, 18 in *Corpus Christianorum* I, 151-153.

[12]Chap. 41; *seven* 'hours' in all: Morning, Terce, Sext, None, Night, Midnight, Cockcrow. Tertullian mentions *five:* Morning, Terce, Sext, None, Evening: *De oratione,* 25, p. 34, and makes somewhat vaguer references to vigils and/or *agapes* celebrated at night: *Apologia,* 39, note 11 *supra; Ad uxorem,* 2, 5 in *Corp. Christ* I, p. 389; *De fuga,* 14, 1 in *Corp. Christ* II, p. 1155. Cyprian, *The Lord's Prayer,* 34-36, has *five* day hours with more insistent references to

praying by night. Clement of Alexandria and Origen seem to have known *six* hours: Jay, *Origen,* pp. 37-38.

[13]Joan Walker, "Terce, Sext and None. An Apostolic Custom," *Studia Patristica* 5 (1962), pp. 206-212, insists that the peculiar chronology of the passion in Mark's Gospel (ca. 65 A.D.) "reflects both the catechetical and liturgical interests of the Church of Rome."

[14]Patristic Testimony: Eusebius of Caesarea (ca. 260-339), *Commentary on Ps. 64:* 10 in PG 23, 640; *On Psalm 91* in PG 23, 1172 and *On Psalm 148:8* in PG 24, 49; Epiphanius of Salamis (ca. 315-403), *Against Heresies* III, 23 in PG 42, 829; Athanasius of Alexandria (ca. 296-373), *On Virginity,* 12-20 ed. E. F. von der Goltz, *Texte unter Untersuchungen* 29 (Leipzig, 1905), pp. 45-56; Basil the Great (ca. 330-379), *Letter 207, trans, Sr. Agnes Clare Way, Letters of St. Basil (Fathers of the Church,* 28; New York, 1955), pp. 81-85. Perhaps Basil is speaking more clearly here of an extended Vigil than simply of Vespers, but he has such a Vigil end with Psalm 51, "the psalm of confession," the typical beginning of Matins. He also insists that the customs of his church "are in accord and harmony with those of all the churches of God" (p. 83). In Basil's *Longer Rules,* chap. 37, trans. Sr. M. Monica Wagner *(Frs. of the Church,* 9; N.Y., 1950), pp. 306-311, Matins and Evensong, as two daily members of the seven "times for prayer customarily established in commnities," get no special prominence any more than they do in Jerome, *Letter 22, to Eustochium* when he lists the "regular fixed time for prayers" (trans. Paul Carroll, *The Satirical Letters of St. Jerome* [Chicago, 1956], pp. 60-61); John Chrysostom (ca. 347-407), *Baptismal Instructions* VIII, 17-18, trans. Paul Harkins *(Ancient Christian Writers,* 31; Westminster, Md., 1963), pp. 126-127; *Apostolic Constitutions* (Syria, ca. 380) II, 59; VII, 47-48; VIII, 34-39 *(Ante-Nicene Fathers,* 7, pp. 422-423, 478, 496-497); *Egeria's Travels* (Palestine, 381-384), II, 24, trans. John Wilkinson (London, 1971), pp. 123-124; Augustine of Hippo (354-430), *Confessions* V, 9, 17, in CSEL 33, 104; St. Patrick, I Synod (A.D. 457), canon 7, ed. Ludwig Bieler, *The Irish Penitentials* (Dublin, 1963), p. 54; Hilary of Arles (bp. 429-449), *Commentary on Ps. 112:3* in PL 9, 420.

[15]F. van der Meer, *Augustine the Bishop* (New York, 1961), 172-173, 176-177. At Hippo Eucharist and Vespers were "daily acts of worship" and there may not have been any Matins proper. Evening worship *(lucernarium, vespertinum)* consisted of hymns, psalms and readings, with or without a homily *(tractatio).*

[16]*On the Lord's Prayer,* 35, trans. Deferrari, pp. 157-158.

[17]II, 24, ed. Ephrem Rahmani (Mainz, 1899), p. 145.

[18]Basil, *Longer Rule,* qu. 37, trans. Wagner, p. 309.

[19]Cassian, *Institutes* III, 3 in NPNF 40, 214; Athanasius, *On Virginity,* 16, ed. Von der Goltz, p. 51.

[20]*Testamentum Domini* II, 24, ed. Rahmani, p. 145; Cyprian, *De oratione,* 35, p. 158.

[21]*Apostolic Constitutions VIII, 34-37, p. 496; Basil, Rule,* qu. 37, p. 310

[22]Basil, Rule, *ibid.;* Athanasius, *On Virginity,* 17, ed. Von der Goltz, pp. 51-52; John Chrysostom, *Baptismal Instructions,* VIII, 17-18, trans. Harkins, pp. 126-127.

[23]John Chrysostom, *Homily on Matthew,* 3-4 in PG 58, 644-46; *Apostolic Constitutions* VIII, 35-40, pp. 496-497 (diaconal biddings, episcopal collects).

[24]*Egeria's Travels,* II, 24, trans. Wilkinson, pp. 123-124, speaks of extended responsorial and antiphonal psalmody at Vespers *(psalmi lucernares);* Basil, *Rule,* 37, p. 311, approves of variety and diversity in the prayers and psalms recited at the appointed hours to avoid "routine and boredom" and "distraction."

[25]In some churches appropriate readings were frequent: *Egeria's Travels,* II, 27, 8, p. 130; II, 32, 1, p. 133 and *passim.* For Hippo. see note 15, *supra.*

[26]*Egeria's Travels* II, 24, trans. Wilkinson. p. 124-125; *Apostolic Constitutions,* II, 58, 2-4 in ANF VII, 422-423; cf. Juan Mateos, S.J., "La vigile cathédrale chez Egérie," *Orientalia Christiana Perodica* 28 (1961) 281-312.

[27]Mateos' most accessible articles (in English) are: "The Origins of the Divine Office," *Worship* 41, 8 (Oct. 1967) 477-485 and "The Morning and Evening Office," *Worship* 42, 1 (Jan. 1968) 31-47.

[28]Taft: "Thanksgiving for the Light. Toward a Theology of Vespers," *Diakonia* 13 (1978) 27-50.

[29]Winkler: "Das Offizium am Ende des 4 Jahrhunderts und das heutige chaldäische Offizium: ihr strukturellen Zusammenhange," *Ostkirchliche Studien* 19 (1970) 89-311 and "Uber die Kathedralvesper in den verschiedenen Riten des Ostens und Westens," *Archiv für Liturgiewissenschaft* 16 (1974) 53-102.

Morning Praise

Morning Praise

SERVICE
NOTES ## Opening

We begin Morning Prayer and a fresh day with a pivotal line from Psalm 50/51 asking the Lord to enable us to offer fitting praise to the triune God. Our model morning hymn is a metrical version of Psalm 94/95 (*Venite*) which has been used as a call to prayer at least since the time of St. Benedict of Nursia (+555). Almost all modern Offices employ this psalm as an introduction to daily worship.

In a larger, more formal setting the ministers may enter in procession: a thurifer with incense, a reader with the Scriptures, cantor and leader. In more informal settings, the ministers may take their places as the congregation gathers.

Psalmody

In the Christian tradition the morning psalms *par excellence* have been Psalms 50/51 and 62/63. Here Psalm 62/63 is assigned to most mornings while Psalm 50/51 is reserved for Wednesdays and Fridays and other penitential days (e.g. Lent). This is a small attempt to restore the rhythm of the Christian week: Wednesday and Friday, days of the Passion; Sunday, day of the Resurrection.

Psalms of Praise or Old Testament Canticles of Praise may be added to Psalms 50/51 and 62/63. These hymns of praise gave Morning Prayer its older name of Lauds.

The Word of God

The reader goes to the lectern to proclaim the Word of God, even when it is only a brief selection.

For longer readings, see the Appendix or other standard lectionaries. Some groups may prefer to read the Bible in course.

On special occasions, additional readings and a brief homily may be appropriate.

Canticle of Praise

At this point in the service a climactic song characteristic of New Testament worship is sung. Western churches normally use the Canticle of Zachary or the *Te Deum*; Eastern churches the Great Doxology (*Gloria in Excelsis*). These songs are sung standing and may be accompanied by a morning oblation of incense to symbolize our prayer and the intercession of the saints. Such a commemoration of the sisters and brothers who have gone before us gives the morning Office an eschatalogical flavor, helping us to rejoice in the on-coming Parousia.

Petitions

Morning Prayer draws to a close with a special unit of prayer *(preces)* characteristic of the Latin Offices: Lord's Prayer, chosen versicles from the psalms, concluding prayer.

Other forms of intercessory prayer may be substituted, if desired.

Conclusion

The community is dismissed with a simple blessing.

Morning Praise

MUSICAL SETTING: DAVID CLARK ISELE

OPENING Introduction

All Stand *All make a sign of the cross on their lips as the leader sings:*

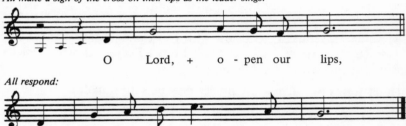

O Lord, + o - pen our lips,

All respond:

And we shall de - clare your praise.

Morning Hymn

Psalm 95
Trans., James Quinn, S.J., 1969

1. To God with glad - ness sing, your
2. He cra - dles in his hand the
3. Your heav'n - ly Fa - ther praise, ac -

1. Rock and Sa - vior bless; With -
2. heights and depths of earth; He
3. claim his on - ly Son, Your

22

1. in his tem - ple bring your songs of
2. made the sea and land, he brought the
3. voice in hom - age raise to him who

1. thank - ful - ness! O God of
2. world to birth! O God most
3. makes all one! O Dove of

1. might, to you we sing, En -
2. high, we are your sheep, On
3. peace, on us des - cend, That

1. throned as King on hea - ven's height!
2. us you keep your Shep - herd's eye!
3. strife may end and joy in - crease!

23

PSALMODY Psalm 62/63: Longing for God in the Shadow of the Cross

All are seated *The psalms in this service are sung in a responsorial manner, i.e., the cantor sings the antiphon and all repeat it; then the cantor sings the verses of the psalm and all repeat the antiphon as indicated.*

Antiphon I

In the morn - ing I will sing ____ will

sing glad songs of praise to you.

Antiphon II

In the shad - ow of your wings I sing for joy.

1. Oh God you are my God and I long for you from ear-ly morn-ing. _____ My whole be-ing de-sires you like a dry worn out and wa-ter-less land, my soul is thirst-y for you.

Antiphon

2. Let me see you in the sanc-tu-a-ry; let me see how might-y and glo-ri-ous you are. Your con-stant love is bet-ter than life it-self, and so I will praise you.

Antiphon

3. I will give you thanks as long as I live; I will raise my hands to you in prayer. My soul will feast and be sat - is - fied, and I will sing glad songs of praise to you.

Antiphon

4. As I lie in bed I re - mem-ber you; all night long I think of you, be - cause you have al-ways been my help. In the

shad - ow of your wings I sing for joy. I cling to you, and your hands keep me safe.

Antiphon

5. Glo - ry to the Fa - ther, and to the Son, and

to the Ho - ly Spir - it: as it was in the be-gin-ning, is

now, and will be for ev - er. A - men.

Antiphon

Psalm Prayer

The leader invites everyone to pray in silence for a moment:
Let us pray.

Then the leader offers the following psalm prayer in the name of the community:
Father,
Source of unfailing light,
from early morning
we seek you in your sanctuary,
for your love is better than life itself.
As we lift our hands to you in prayer
and our hearts in songs of praise,
may our worship glorify you
and our lives be spent in your service;
through Jesus Christ our Lord.

All:
Amen.

Psalm 50/51: David's Act of Contrition

On Wednesday, Friday and other penitential days, Psalm 50/51 may be used in place of Psalm 62/63.

Antiphon

The sac - ri - fice you ac - cept, O God, is a

hum - ble spir - it.

Verses

1. Have mercy on me, O God, in your lov - ing kindness;
2. I know full well my mis - deeds,
3. You look for truth in my in - most being,
4. Create in me a pure heart, O God,
5. Deliver me from death, O God my savior,
6. You have no delight in sacrifices;
7. Glory to the Father, and to the Son,

1. in your com - passion blot out my of - fen - ses.
2. and my sin is ever be - fore me.
3. and teach me wisdom in my heart.
4. and re - new a right spirit with - in me.
5. that my tongue may sing of your jus - tice.
6. a burnt - offering from me would not please you,
7. and to the Holy Spir - it,

28

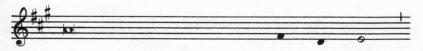

1. Wash me thoroughly from my in - iquity,
2. Against you, against you only, have I sinned,
3. Purify me that I may be clean,
4. Cast me not away from your presence,
5. O Lord, o - pen my lips,
6. The sacrifice you accept is a hum - ble spirit;
7. As it was in the be - ginning,

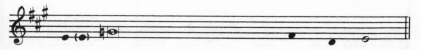

1. and cleanse me from my sin.
2. and done what is evil in your sight.
3. wash me, make me whit - er than snow.
4, and take not your holy Spir - it from me.
5. and my mouth shall pro - claim your praise.
6. a broken, contrite heart you will not re - ject.
7. is now, and will be for ev - er. A - men.

Psalm Prayer

The leader invites everyone to pray in silence for a moment:
Let us pray.

Then the leader offers the following psalm prayer in the name of the community:
Almighty and merciful Father,
you freely forgive those who confess their sins,
as did David, the prophet-king of Israel.
We acknowledge our offenses before you.
Restore the joy of our salvation,
and wash away all our sins
in the precious blood of your beloved Son,
our Savior Jesus Christ,
who lives and reigns with you and the Holy Spirit,
one God, for ever and ever.

All:
Amen.

Psalm 150: The Grand Doxology

All stand *Psalm 150, an Old Testament Canticle or one of the other Psalms of Praise (145/146-149) may be sung at this point.*

Trans., James Quinn, S.J., 1969

1. Blest   be   the   Lord   our   God!   With
2. All   that   has   life   and   breath,   Give

1. joy   let heav - en   ring;   Be - fore   his pres - ence
2. thanks with heart - felt   songs !   To   him   let   all   cre -

1. let   all   the   earth   it's   songs   of   hom - age
2. a -   tion   sing   to   whom all   praise   be -

1. bring! His might - y deeds be told; His
2. longs! Ac - claim the Fa - ther's love; Who

1. ma - jes - ty be praised; To
2. gave us Christ his Son! Praise,

1. God en - throned in heav'n - ly light
2. too, the Spir - it giv'n by both,

let ev - 'ry voice be raised!
with both for - ev - er one!

There is no psalm prayer after this psalm.

THE WORD
OF GOD Reading

All are seated   *A reader proclaims the word of God:*

Listen, Israel: the Lord is our God, the Lord alone.
You shall love the Lord your God with all your heart,
with all your soul, with all your strength.
Let these words I urge on you today be written on your heart.
You shall repeat them to your children
and say them over to them whether at rest in your house or walking
   abroad,
at your lying down or at your rising.
For you are a people consecrated to the Lord your God;
it is you that the Lord our God has chosen to be his very own people
out of all the peoples of the earth. *(Deut. 6:4-9; 7:6)*

At the end of the reading, the reader raises the Bible and says:

This is the word of the Lord.

All respond:

Thanks be to God.

After the reading, all pray in silence opening their minds and hearts to the Spirit.

Other brief readings:

Deuteronomy 4:39-40
Isaiah 55:1-3
1 Thessalonians 5:2-10
2 Thessalonians 3:6-13
Romans 12:9-13
Romans 12:14-21
Romans 13:8-10
Romans 13:11-13
2 Timothy 2:1-7

Canticle of Zachary (Lk. 1:67-79)

During this song, the altar and the community may be honored with incense. All make a sign **All stand**
of the cross as the canticle begins:

Trans., James Quinn, S.J., 1975

1. Bless'd be + the God of Is - ra - el, The
2. Through ho - ly pro-phets did he speak His
3. Of old he gave his sol - emn oath To
4. O ti - ny child your name shall be The
5. The ris - ing sun shall shine on us To

1. ev - er - liv - ing Lord,
2. word in days of old,
3. Fa - ther A - bra - ham;
4. pro - phet of the Lord;
5. bring the light of day

33

1. Who comes in pow'r to save his own, His
2. That he would save us from our foes And
3. His seed a might - y race should be And
4. The way of God you shall pre - pare To
5. To all who sit in dark - est night And

1. peo - ple Is - ra - el.
2. all who bear us ill.
3. bless'd for - ev - er more.
4. make his com - ing known.
5. sha - dow of the grave.

1. For Is - ra - el he rai - ses up, Sal -
2. To our an - ces - tors did he give His
3. He vowed to set his peo - ple free From
4. You shall pro-claim to Is - ra - el Sal -
5. Our foot - steps God shall safe - ly guide To

1. In   Da - vid's house who   reigned   as   king   And
2. So   with   us   all   he   keeps   his   word   In
3. That   we   might serve him   all   our   days   In
4. When   God   shall wipe   a - way   all   sins   In
5. His   name   for - ev - er - more   be   bless'd   Who

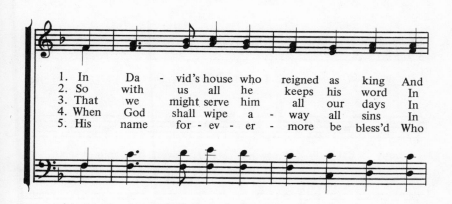

1. va   - tion's tow'r   on   high
2. co   - ve - nant   of   love;
3. fear   of   ev - 'ry   foe,
4. va   - tion's dawn - ing   day,
5. walk   the   ways   of   peace.

1. ser   - vant   of   the   Lord.
2. love   that   knows   no   end.
3. good - ness,   love   and   peace.
4. his   re - deem - ing   love.
5. lives   and   loves   and   saves.

PETITIONS The Lord's Prayer

Leader:

Now let us pray as Christ the Lord has taught us:

All may extend their hands as they pray:

Our Fa-ther in heav-en, hal-lowed be your name,

your king-dom come, your will be done,

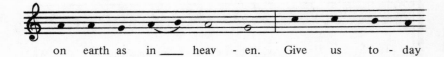

on earth as in ___ heav-en. Give us to-day

our dai-ly bread. For-give us our sins

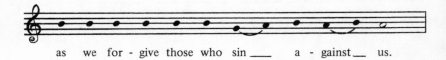

as we for-give those who sin ___ a-gainst ___ us.

Save us from the time of trial and de-liv-er

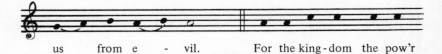

us from e-vil. For the king-dom the pow'r

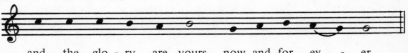

and the glo-ry are yours, now and for ev-er.

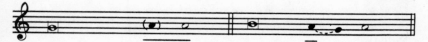

Cantor:
In you, O Lord, is the source of <u>life</u>.

All:
In your light we shall <u>see</u> light.

Cantor:
Send forth your light and your <u>truth</u>.

All:
Let these be <u>our</u> guide.

Cantor:
Fill us each morning with your constant <u>love</u>.

All:
That we may sing and be glad all <u>our</u> life.

Cantor:
Let us see your mighty <u>acts</u>.

All:
May your children see your glori<u>ous</u> might.

Cantor:
Lord our God, may your blessing be up<u>on us</u>.

All:
And give us success in all <u>we</u> do.

In silent or spontaneous prayer, all bring before God the concerns of a new day.

Concluding Prayer

The leader brings the petitions to a close with an appropriate prayer:

Sunday
Father of light,
yours is the morning
and yours is the evening.
Let Christ, the Sun of Justice,
shine for ever in our hearts
and draw us to that light
where you live in radiant glory.
We ask this through Jesus the Lord.

All:
Amen.

Friday
Almighty God and Father,
your beloved Son willingly endured
the agony and shame of the cross for our redemption.
Give us the courage to take up our cross
and follow him in newness of life and hope.
He lives and reigns with you and the Holy Spirit,
one God, now and for ever.

All:
Amen.

Weekdays
All-powerful and ever-living God,
shine with the light of your radiance
on a people who live in the shadow of death.
Let the dawn from on high break upon us:
your Son our Lord Jesus Christ,
who lives and reigns with you and the Holy Spirit,
one God, for ever and ever.

All:
Amen.

Blessing CLOSING

The leader invokes God's blessing on the assembled people and sends them out to their day's work:

Let us bless the Lord.

All:

And give him thanks.

Leader:

May the Lord almighty + bless our days and our deeds with his peace.

All:

Amen.

Morning Praise

MUSICAL SETTING: HOWARD HUGHES, SM

OPENING Introduction

All stand *All make a sign of the cross on their lips as the leader sings:*

O Lord, + o - pen our lips,

All respond:

And we shall de - clare your praise.

Equal Voices:

And we shall de - clare your praise.

SATB

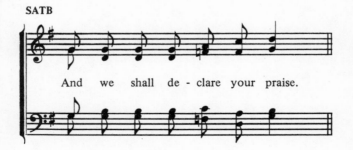

And we shall de - clare your praise.

Morning Hymn

Psalm 95
Trans., James Quinn, S.J., 1969

1. To God with glad - ness sing, Your
2. He cra - dles in his hand The
3. Your heav - 'nly Fa - ther praise, Ac -

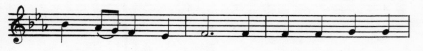

1. Rock and Sav - ior bless; With - in his tem - ple
2. heights and depths of earth; He made the sea and
3. claim his on - ly Son, Your voice in hom - age

1. bring Your songs of thank - ful - ness! O
2. land, He brought the world to birth! O
3. raise To him who makes all one! O

1. God of might, To you we sing, En -
2. God most high, We are your sheep; On
3. Dove of peace, On us de - scend That

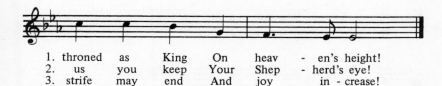

1. throned as King On heav - en's height!
2. us you keep Your Shep - herd's eye!
3. strife may end And joy in - crease!

PSALMODY Psalm 62/63: Longing for God in the Shadow of the Cross

All are seated *The psalms in this service are sung in a responsorial manner, i.e., the cantor sings the antiphon and all repeat it; then the cantor sings the verses of the psalm and all repeat the antiphon as indicated.*

Antiphon I

In the shad - ow of your wings I sing for joy.

Antiphon II

In the morn - ing I will sing glad songs of praise to you.

Verses

1) O God, you are my God, and I long for you from ear - ly morn - ing. My whole be - ing de - sires you; like a dry, worn-out and waterless land, my soul is thirst - y for you. *Antiphon*

2) Let me see you in the sanc - tu - ar - y;

let me see how might - y and glo - rious you are.

Your con - stant love is bet - ter than life it - self,

and so I will praise you. 3) I will give you thanks as long as I live;
Antiphon

I will raise my hands to you in prayer.

My soul will feast and be sat - is - fied,

and I will sing glad songs of praise to you.
Antiphon

43

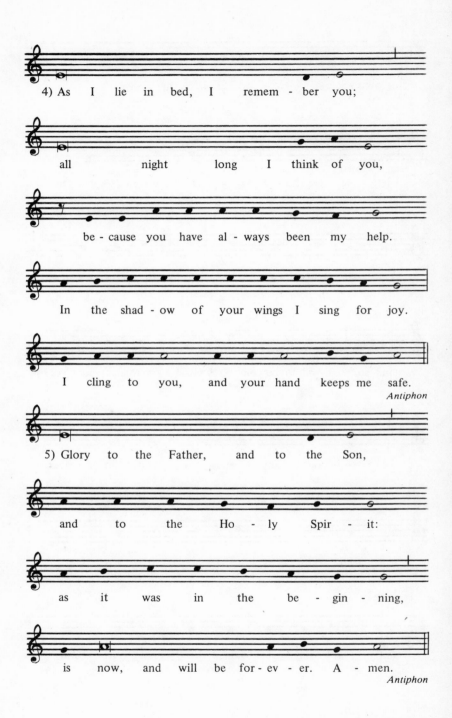

4) As I lie in bed, I remem - ber you;

all night long I think of you,

be - cause you have al - ways been my help.

In the shad - ow of your wings I sing for joy.

I cling to you, and your hand keeps me safe.

Antiphon

5) Glory to the Father, and to the Son,

and to the Ho - ly Spir - it:

as it was in the be - gin - ning,

is now, and will be for - ev - er. A - men.

Antiphon

Psalm Prayer

The leader invites everyone to pray in silence for a moment:
Let us pray.

Then the leader offers the following psalm prayer in the name of the community:
Father,
Source of unfailing light,
from early morning
we seek you in your sanctuary,
for your love is better than life itself.
As we lift our hands to you in prayer
and our hearts in songs of praise,
may our worship glorify you
and our lives be spent in your service;
through Jesus Christ our Lord.

All:
Amen.

Psalm 50/51: David's Act of Contrition

*On Wednesday, Friday and other penitential days, Psalm 50/51 may be used in place of Psalm
62/63.*

Antiphon

The sac - ri - fice you ac - cept, O God, is a

hum - ble spir - it.

Verses

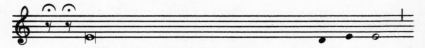

1. Have mercy on me, O God, in your lov - ing kind - ness;

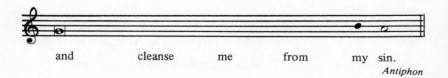

in your compassion blot out my of - fen - ses.

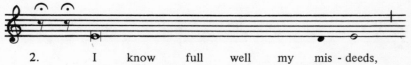

Wash me thoroughly from my in - i - qui - ty,

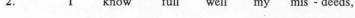

and cleanse me from my sin.

Antiphon

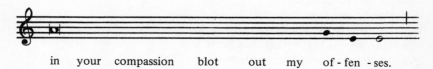

2. I know full well my mis - deeds,

and my sin is ever be - fore me.

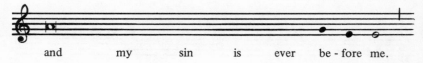

Against you, against you only, have I sinned,

and done what is evil in your sight.

Antiphon

3. Yet you look for truth in my in-most be-ing,

and teach me wisdom in my heart.

Purify me that I may be clean,

wash me, make me whiter than snow.

Antiphon

4. Create in me a pure heart, O God,

and renew a right spirit with-in me.

Cast me not away from your pres-ence,

and take not your holy Spirit from me.

Antiphon

5. Deliver me from death, O God my sav - ior,

that my tongue may sing of your jus - tice.

O Lord, open my lips,

and my mouth shall proclaim your praise.

Antiphon

6. You have no delight in sac - fi - fic - es;

a burnt - offering from me would not please you.

The sacrifice you accept is a hum-ble spir - it;

a broken and contrite heart, O God, you will not re - ject.

Antiphon

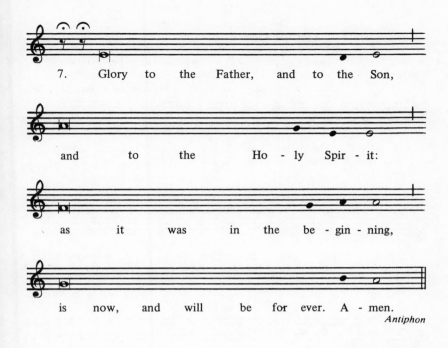

7. Glory to the Father, and to the Son,

and to the Ho - ly Spir - it:

as it was in the be - gin - ning,

is now, and will be for ever. A - men.

Antiphon

Psalm Prayer

The leader invites everyone to pray in silence for a moment:

Let us pray.

Then the leader offers the following psalm prayer in the name of the community:

Almighty and merciful Father,
you freely forgive those who confess their sins,
as did David, the prophet-king of Israel.
We acknowledge our offenses before you.
Restore the joy of our salvation,
and wash away all our sins
in the precious blood of your beloved Son,
our Savior Jesus Christ,
who lives and reigns with you and the Holy Spirit,
one God, for ever and ever.

All:

Amen.

Psalm 150: The Grand Doxology

All stand *Psalm 150, an Old Testament Canticle or one of the other Psalms of Praise (145/146-149) may be sung at this point.*

Trans., James Quinn, S.J., 1969

1. Bless'd be the Lord our God! With joy let heav - en ring; Be - fore his pres - ence let all the earth Its songs of hom - age bring! His might - y deeds be told; His maj - es - ty be praised; To God en - throned in heav - 'nly light Let ev - 'ry voice be raised!

2. All that has life and breath, Give thanks with heart - felt songs! To him let all cre - a - tion sing To whom all praise be longs! Ac - claim the Fa - ther's love, Who gave us Christ his Son; Praise, too, the Spir - it, giv'n by both, With both for - ev - er one!

50   *There is no psalm prayer after this psalm.*

THE WORD
Reading OF GOD

A reader proclaims the word of God: All are seated

Listen, Israel: the Lord is our God, the Lord alone.
You shall love the Lord your God with all your heart,
with all your soul, with all your strength.
Let these words I urge on you today be written on your heart.
You shall repeat them to your children
and say them over to them whether at rest in your house or walking
  abroad,
at your lying down or at your rising.
For you are a people consecrated to the Lord your God;
it is you that the Lord our God has chosen to be his very own people
out of all the peoples of the earth. *(Deut. 6:4-9; 7:6)*

At the end of the reading, the reader raises the Bible and says:
This is the word of the Lord.

All respond:
Thanks be to God.

After the reading, all pray in silence opening their minds and hearts to the Spirit.

Other brief readings:

Deuteronomy 4:39-40
Isaiah 55:1-3
1 Thessalonians 5:2-10
2 Thessalonians 3:6-13
Romans 12:9-13
Romans 12:14-21
Romans 13:8-10
Romans 13:11-13
2 Timothy 2:1-7

CANTICLE
OF PRAISE Canticle of Zachary (Lk. 1:67-79)

All stand *During this song, the altar and the community may be honored with incense. All make a sign of the cross as the canticle begins:*

Trans. James Quinn, S.J., 1975

1. Bless'd be + the God of Is - ra - el, The
2. Through ho - ly proph - ets did he speak His
3. Of old he gave his sol - emn oath To
4. O ti - ny child, your name shall be The
5. The ris - ing sun shall shine on us To

1. ev - er - liv -ing Lord, Who comes in pow'r to save his own, His
2. word in days of old, That he would save us from our foes And
3. fa - ther A - bra - ham; His seed a might-y race should be And
4. proph-et of the Lord: The way of God you shall pre-pare To
5. bring the light of day To all who sit in dark-est night And

1. peo - ple Is - ra - el. For Is - ra - el he
2. all who bear us ill. To our an - ces - tors
3. bless'd for ev - er - more. He vowed to set his
4. make his com - ing known. You shall pro-claim to
5. shad - ow of the grave. Our foot-steps God shall

1. rais - es up Sal - va - tion's tow'r on high In
2. did he give His cov - e - nant of love; So
3. peo - ple free From fear of ev - 'ry foe, That
4. Is - ra - el Sal - va - tion's dawn-ing day, When
5. safe - ly guide To walk the ways of peace. His

1. Da - vid's house who reigned as king And ser-vant of the Lord.
2. with us all he keeps his word In love that knows no end.
3. we might serve him all our days In good-ness, love and peace.
4. God shall wipe a - way our sins In his re - deem-ing love.
5. name for ev - er - more be bless'd Who lives and loves and saves.

52

The Lord's Prayer PETITIONS

Leader:

Now let us pray as Christ the Lord has taught us:

All may extend their hands as they pray:

Our Fa - ther in heav - en, hal - lowed be your name,

your king - dom come, your will be done,

on earth as in ___ heav - en. Give us to - day

our dai - ly bread. For - give us our sins

as we for - give those who sin ___ a - gainst ___ us.

Save us from the time of trial and de - liv - er

us from e - vil. For the king - dom the pow'r

and the glo - ry are yours, now and for ev - er.

53

Versicles

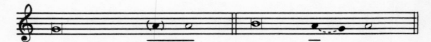

Cantor:
In you, O Lord, is the source of <u>life</u>.

All:
In your light we shall <u>see</u> light.

Cantor:
Send forth your light and your <u>truth</u>.

All:
Let these be <u>our</u> guide.

Cantor:
Fill us each morning with your constant <u>love</u>.

All:
That we may sing and be glad all <u>our</u> life.

Cantor:
Let us see your mighty <u>acts</u>.

All:
May your children see your glo<u>rious</u> might.

Cantor:
Lord our God, may your blessing be up<u>on us</u>.

All:
And give us success in all <u>we</u> do.

In silent or spontaneous prayer, all bring before God the concerns of a new day.

Concluding Prayer

The leader brings the petitions to a close with an appropriate prayer:
Sunday
Father of light,
yours is the morning
and yours is the evening.
Let Christ, the Sun of Justice,
shine for ever in our hearts
and draw us to that light
where you live in radiant glory.
We ask this through Jesus the Lord.

All:
Amen.

Friday
Almighty God and Father,
your beloved Son willingly endured
the agony and shame of the cross for our redemption.
Give us the courage to take up our cross
and follow him in newness of life and hope.
He lives and reigns with you and the Holy Spirit,
one God, now and for ever.

All:
Amen.

Weekdays
All-powerful and ever-living God,
shine with the light of your radiance
on a people who live in the shadow of death.
Let the dawn from on high break upon us:
your Son our Lord Jesus Christ,
who lives and reigns with you and the Holy Spirit,
one God, for ever and ever.

All:
Amen.

Blessing CLOSING

The leader invokes God's blessing on the assembled people and sends them out to their day's work:
Let us bless the Lord.

All:
And give him thanks.

Leader:
May the Lord almighty + bless our days and our deeds with his peace.

All:
Amen.

Morning Praise

MUSICAL SETTING: MICHAEL JONCAS

OPENING Introduction

All stand *All make a sign of the cross on their lips as the leader sings:*

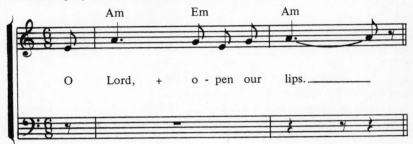

O Lord, + o-pen our lips.

All respond:

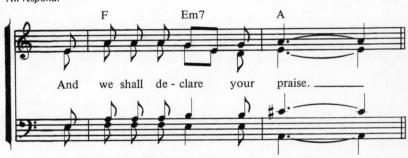

And we shall de-clare your praise.

Morning Hymn

Psalm 95
Trans., James Quinn, S.J., 1969

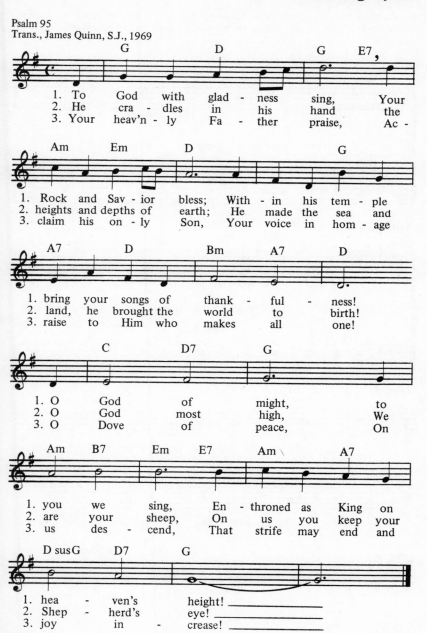

1. To God with glad - ness sing, Your
2. He cra - dles in his hand the
3. Your heav'n - ly Fa - ther praise, Ac -

1. Rock and Sav - ior bless; With - in his tem - ple
2. heights and depths of earth; He made the sea and
3. claim his on - ly Son, Your voice in hom - age

1. bring your songs of thank - ful - ness!
2. land, he brought the world to birth!
3. raise to Him who makes all one!

1. O God of might, to
2. O God most high, We
3. O Dove of peace, On

1. you we sing, En - throned as King on
2. are your sheep, On us you keep your
3. us des - cend, That strife may end and

1. hea - ven's height! _____
2. Shep - herd's eye! _____
3. joy in - crease! _____

57

PSALMODY Psalm 62/63: Longing for God in the Shadow of the Cross

All are seated *The psalms in this service are sung in a responsorial manner, i.e., the cantor sings the antiphon and all repeat it; then the cantor sings the verses of the psalm and all repeat the antiphon as indicated.*

Antiphon I

In the sha-dow of your wings I sing for joy.

Antiphon II

In the morn-ing I will sing glad songs of praise to you.

Verses

1. O— God, you are my God, and I long for you from

ear-ly— morn-ing; My whole being

de-sires— you; like a dry, worn-out

and wa-ter-less land, my soul is thirst-y for you.

Antiphon

58

2. Let me see you in the sanc - tu - ar - y;

let me see how mighty and glo - ri - ous you are.

Your constant love is better than life it - self,

and so I will praise___ you.

Antiphon

3. I will give you thanks as long ___ as I live;

I will raise my hands to you _____ in prayer.

My soul will feast and be sat - is - fied,

and I will sing glad songs of praise to you.

Antiphon

59

E   Am   E

4. As I lie in bed, I re-mem - ber you;

E   Am   E

all night long I think of you, because you have al -ways been my help.

F#m   B7   Am

In the shadow of your wings I sing for joy. I cling to you,

E

and your hand keeps me safe. *Antiphon*

E   Am   E

5. Glo - ry to the Father, and to the Son,

Am   E

and to the Ho - ly Spir - it:

F#m   B7

as it was in the be - gin - ning, is now,

Am   E

and will be forever. A - men. *Antiphon*

Psalm Prayer

The leader invites everyone to pray in silence for a moment:
Let us pray.

Then the leader offers the following psalm prayer in the name of the community:
Father,
Source of unfailing light,
from early morning
we seek you in your sanctuary,
for your love is better than life itself.
As we lift our hands to you in prayer
and our hearts in songs of praise,
may our worship glorify you
and our lives be spent in your service;
through Jesus Christ our Lord.
All:
Amen.

Psalm 50/51: David's Act of Contrition

On Wednesday, Friday and other penitential days, Psalm 50/51 may be used in place of Psalm 62/63.

Antiphon

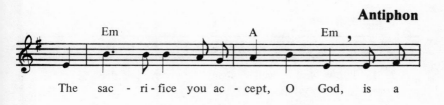

The sac - ri - fice you ac - cept, O God, is a

hum - ble spir - it,

Verses

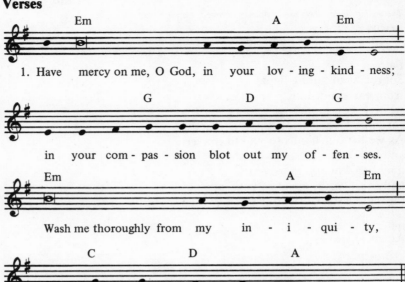

1. Have mercy on me, O God, in your lov - ing - kind - ness;

in your com - pas - sion blot out my of - fen - ses.

Wash me thoroughly from my in - i - qui - ty,

and cleanse me from my sin.

Antiphon

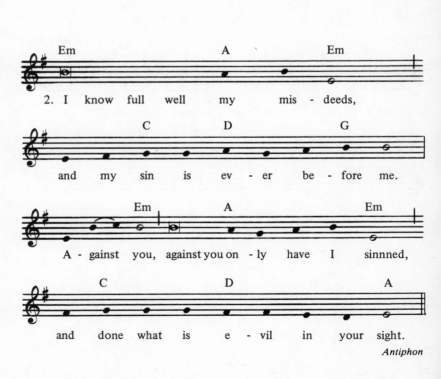

2. I know full well my mis - deeds,

and my sin is ev - er be - fore me.

A - gainst you, against you on - ly have I sinnned,

and done what is e - vil in your sight.

Antiphon

62

3. Yet you look for truth in my in-most be-ing,

and teach me wis-dom in my heart.

Purify me that I may be clean,

wash me, make me whit-er than snow.

Antiphon

4. Create in me a pure___ heart, O God,

and re-new a right spir-it with-in me.

Cast me not away from your pres-ence,

and take not your ho-ly Spir-it from me.

Antiphon

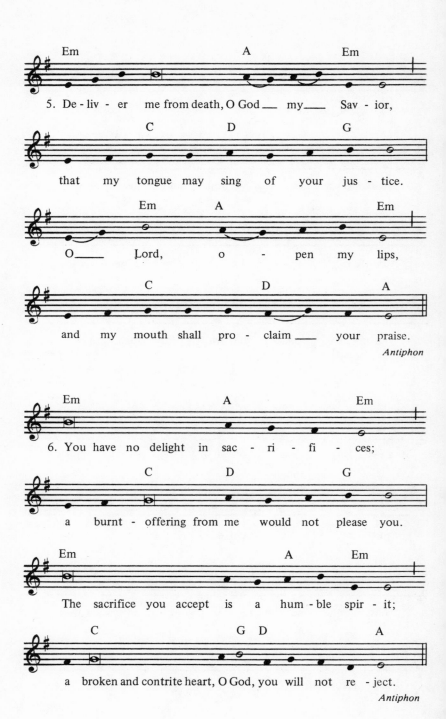

Em   **A**   **Em**

5. De - liv - er   me from death, O God ___ my ___ Sav - ior,

C   **D**   **G**

that   my   tongue may   sing   of   your   jus - tice.

Em   **A**   **Em**

O ___ Lord,   o -   pen   my   lips,

C   **D**   **A**

and   my   mouth shall pro - claim ___ your praise.

Antiphon

Em   **A**   **Em**

6. You have no delight in sac - ri - fi - ces;

C   **D**   **G**

a   burnt - offering from me   would not   please you.

Em   **A**   **Em**

The sacrifice you accept is   a   hum - ble spir - it;

C   **G** **D**   **A**

a broken and contrite heart, O God, you will not re - ject.

Antiphon

64

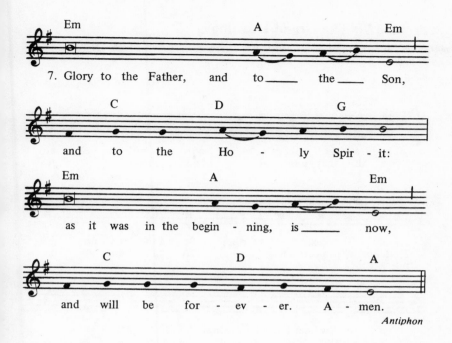

7. Glory to the Father,   and   to____   the ____ Son,

and   to   the   Ho - ly   Spir - it:

as it was in the begin - ning, is____   now,

and   will   be   for - ev - er.   A - men.

Antiphon

Psalm Prayer

The leader invites everyone to pray in silence for a moment:
Let us pray.

Then the leader offers the following psalm prayer in the name of the community:
Almighty and merciful Father,
you freely forgive those who confess their sins,
as did David, the prophet-king of Israel.
We acknowledge our offenses before you.
Restore the joy of our salvation,
and wash away all our sins
in the precious blood of your beloved Son,
our Savior Jesus Christ,
who lives and reigns with you and the Holy Spirit,
one God, for ever and ever.

All:
Amen.

Psalm 150: The Grand Doxology

All stand *Psalm 150, an Old Testament Canticle or one of the other Psalms of Praise (145/146-149) may be sung at this point.*

Trans., James Quinn, S.J., 1969

1. Blest be the Lord, our God! with
2. All that has life and breath, give

1. joy let heav - en ring; Be - fore his pres - ence
2. thanks with heart - felt songs To him let all cre -

1. let all the earth its songs of hom - age bring!
2. a - tion sing to whom all praise be - longs!

1. His might - y deeds be told; his
2. Ac - claim the Fa - ther's love, who

1. ma - jes - ty be praised; To God en-throned in
2. gave us Christ his Son; Praise, too, the Spir - it

1. heav'n - ly light let ev - 'ry voice be raised, let
2. giv'n by both, with both for - ev - er one, with

1. ev - 'ry voice be raised!
2. both for - ev - er - one!

66 *There is no psalm prayer after this psalm.*

A reader proclaims the word of God.

Listen, Israel: the Lord is our God, the Lord alone.
You shall love the Lord your God with all your heart,
with all your soul, with all your strength.
Let these words I urge on you today be written on your heart.
You shall repeat them to your children
and say them over to them whether at rest in your house or walking
   abroad,
at your lying down or at your rising.
For you are a people consecrated to the Lord your God;
it is you that the Lord our God has chosen to be his very own people
out of all the peoples of the earth. *(Deut. 6:4-9; 7:6)*

At the end of the reading, the reader raises the Bible and says:
This is the word of the Lord.

All respond:
Thanks be to God.

After the reading, all pray in silence opening their minds and hearts to the Spirit.

Other brief readings:

Deuteronomy 4:39-40
Isaiah 55:1-3
1 Thessalonians 5:2-10
2 Thessalonians 3:6-13
Romans 12:9-13
Romans 12:14-21
Romans 13:8-10
Romans 13:11-13
2 Timothy 2:1-7

CANTICLE
OF PRAISE Canticle of Zachary (Lk. 1:67-79)

All stand *During this song the altar and the community may be honored with incense. All make a sign of the cross as the canticle begins:*

FOREST GREEN
Trad. English Melody
Arr. R. Vaughan Williams, 1872-1958
Guitar Chords. M.J.
Trans., James Quinn, S.J., 1975

Capo 5

F (C)   Bb (F)   Am (Em)   D7 (A7)

1. Bless'd + be the God of Is - ra - el, The
2. Through ho - ly pro - phets did he speak His
3. Of old he gave his sol - emn oath To
4. O ti - ny child, your name shall be The
5. The ris - ing sun shall shine on us To

Gm (Dm)   C7 (G7)   F (C)

1. ev - er - liv - ing Lord,
2. word in days of old,
3. Fa - ther A - bra - ham;
4. pro - phet of the Lord;
5. bring the light of day

F (C)   Bb (F)   Am (Em)   D7 (A7)

1. Who comes in pow'r to save his own, His
2. That he would save us from our foes And
3. His seed a might - y race should be And
4. The way of God you shall pre - pare To
5. To all who sit in dark - est night And

68

N.B. The guitar chords and written harmonization are not compatible.
Harmonization from The English Hymnal by permission of Oxford University Press

F (C)   B♭ (F)   Am (Em)   D7 (A7)

1. In   Da - vid's house who   reigned as   king   And
2. So   with   us   all   he   keeps his   word   In
3. That   we   might serve him   all   our   days   In
4. When   God   shall wipe a - way   all   sins   In
5. His   name for   ev - er - more   be bless'd   Who

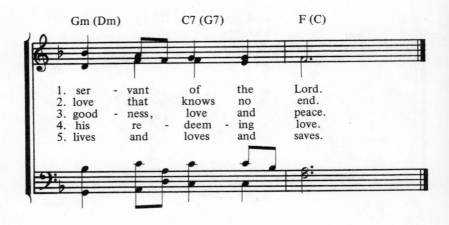

Gm (Dm)   C7 (G7)   F (C)

1. ser - vant   of   the   Lord.
2. love   that   knows no   end.
3. good - ness,   love   and   peace.
4. his   re - deem - ing   love.
5. lives   and   loves and   saves.

Leader:

Now let us pray as Christ the Lord has taught us:

All may extend their hands as they pray:

Our Fa - ther in heav - en, hal - lowed be your name,

your king - dom come, your will be done,

on earth as in ___ heav - en. Give us to - day

our dai - ly bread. For - give us our sins

as we for - give those who sin ___ a - gainst ___ us.

Save us from the time of trial and de - liv - er

us from e - vil. For the king - dom the pow'r

and the glo - ry are yours, now and for ev - er.

Versicles

Cantor:

In you, O Lord, is the source of life.

All:

In your light we shall see light.

Cantor:

Send forth your light and your truth.

All:

Let these be our guide.

Cantor:

Fill us each morning with your constant love.

All:

That we may sing and be glad all our life.

Cantor:

Let us see your mighty acts.

All:

May your children see your glorious might.

Cantor:

Lord our God, may your blessing be upon us.

All:

And give us success in all we do.

In silent or spontaneous prayer, all bring before God the concerns of a new day.

Concluding Prayer

The leader brings the petitions to a close with an appropriate prayer:

Sunday
Father of light,
yours is the morning
and yours is the evening.
Let Christ, the Sun of Justice,
shine for ever in our hearts
and draw us to that light
where you live in radiant glory.
We ask this through Jesus the Lord.

All:

72 Amen.

Friday
Almighty God and Father,
your beloved Son willingly endured
the agony and shame of the cross for our redemption.
Give us the courage to take up our cross
and follow him in newness of life and hope.
He lives and reigns with you and the Holy Spirit,
one God, now and for ever.

All:
Amen.

Weekdays
All-powerful and ever-living God,
shine with the light of your radiance
on a people who live in the shadow of death.
Let the dawn from on high break upon us:
your Son our Lord Jesus Christ,
who lives and reigns with you and the Holy Spirit,
one God, for ever and ever.

All:
Amen.

Blessing CLOSING

The leader invokes God's blessing on the assembled people and sends them out to their day's work.
Let us bless the Lord.

All:
And give him thanks.

Leader:
May the Lord almighty + bless our days and our deeds with his peace.

All:
Amen.

Morning Praise
BRIEF FORM

SERVICE NOTES Morning Prayer is a service of praise to the Creator for the gift of a new day. It serves to consecrate the day, offering to God the work which has begun and praising him for the gift of new light.

The rubrics in the service are to be considered suggestions and should be modified according to the circumstances, such as the place for prayer, size of the group and the time of the Church year.

Opening

The brief opening prayer of praise gives thanks to God for the light of morning.

If the setting for prayer warrants it, there may be a procession including the leader, reader carrying the book of God's word, and song leader.

Psalmody

If at all possible, the psalms are sung. The psalms given are suggestions only. Themes of praise, thanksgiving and creation characterize the psalms prayed in the morning.

It is important that there be a period of silence after the psalm, before the psalm prayer is prayed.

On occasion, during the period of silent reflection, those praying may find it prayerful and beneficial to repeat aloud a phrase from the psalm which has particular meaning for the individual.

It is also possible, on occasion, to use some recordings of the psalms. Recordings of *Biblical Hymns and Psalms* are available from World Library Publications, 5040 North Ravenswood, Chicago, Illinois 60640; the *Gelineau Psalter* is available from G.I.A. Publications, 7404 South Mason Avenue, Chicago, Illinois 60638. Music of the St. Louis Jesuits is available from North American Liturgy Resources, 2110 W. Peoria Avenue, Phoenix, Arizona 85029.

The Word of God

The selections given are suggestions. Various groups may wish to choose their own selections or follow the Table of Longer Readings given in this book or in other publications such as *Daily Bible Reading,* Liturgical Press, Collegeville, Minnesota 56321.

Silent prayer after the reading helps the community to digest the "Bread of the Word." It is possible to have shared reflection after the period of silence or a brief homily.

Song of Praise

The *Gloria in Excelsis* or the Canticle of Zachary is a response of praise to the Word of God. These songs should be sung, rather than recited, if possible.

Standing is recommended for the praise response, if the setting permits it.

Petitions

In morning prayer, the community at prayer asks for God's assistance throughout the day and dedicates the day to the Lord of life.

Various forms for intercessory prayer may be substituted for the single form given here.

The Lord's Prayer

The Lord's Prayer, a summary of the Gospel, concludes the service.

Blessing

A brief blessing is invoked by the leader of prayer. Any suitable short blessing may be used.

A sign of peace may be exchanged, if appropriate.

Morning Praise

BRIEF FORM

OPENING

All stand *All make a sign of the cross as the leader begins:*
Our help is in the name of the Lord,

All respond:
Who made heaven and earth.

The leader prays:
Praise to you, Lord our God,
Ruler of the universe,
Creator of light and darkness,
Giver of peace and Maker of all things.

With compassion, you give light to the earth;
with goodness, you renew the work of creation, day after day.
The earth is full of your riches, O Lord;
in your wisdom, you made them all.

We bless you, Lord our God,
for your gifts, great and small,
for the sun that gives warmth,
for the stars that give light.

May we glorify you with them for ever.

All respond:
Blessed be the Lord, the Giver of light.

One or more morning psalms is prayed.

Psalm 62/63: Longing for God in the Shadow of the Cross

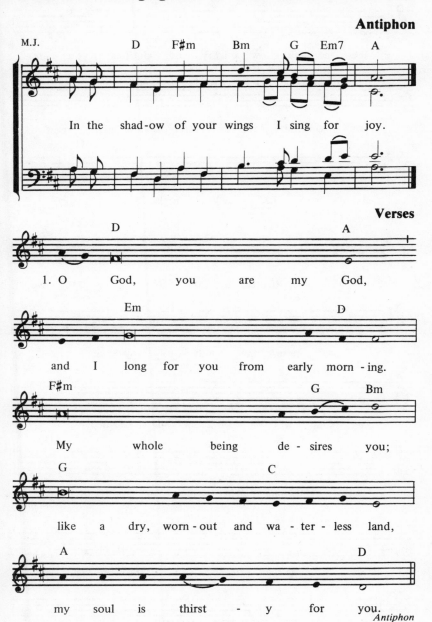

Antiphon

M.J.

In the shad-ow of your wings I sing for joy.

Verses

1. O God, you are my God,

and I long for you from early morn - ing.

My whole being de - sires you;

like a dry, worn - out and wa - ter - less land,

my soul is thirst - y for you.

Antiphon

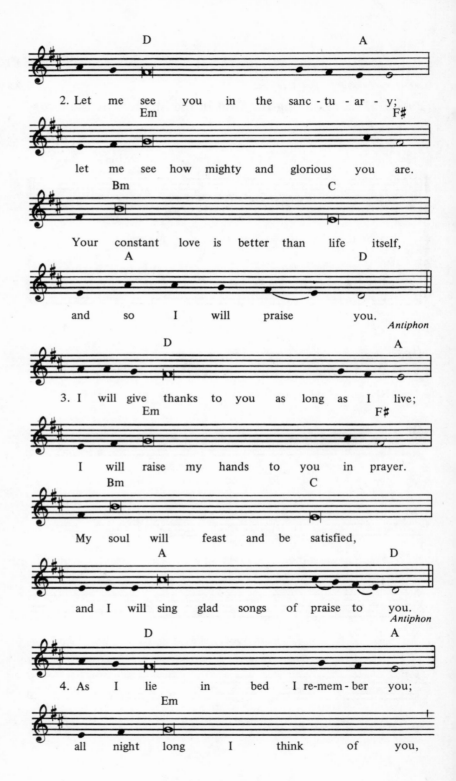

D   A

2. Let me see you in the sanc - tu - ar - y;

Em   F♯

let me see how mighty and glorious you are.

Bm   C

Your constant love is better than life itself,

A   D

and so I will praise you.
Antiphon

D   A

3. I will give thanks to you as long as I live;

Em   F♯

I will raise my hands to you in prayer.

Bm   C

My soul will feast and be satisfied,

A   D

and I will sing glad songs of praise to you.
Antiphon

D   A

4. As I lie in bed I re-mem - ber you;

Em

all night long I think of you,

because you have always been my help.

In the shad-ow of your wings I sing for joy.

I cling to you, and your hand keeps me safe.

Antiphon

5. Glory to the Father, and to the Son,

and to the Ho - ly Spir - it:

as it was in the be - ginning,

is now and will be for ev - er. A - men.

Antiphon

Psalm Prayer

The leader invites everyone to pray in silence for a moment:

Let us pray.

Then the leader offers the following psalm prayer in the name of the community:

From early morning, O God, Source of light,
we seek you in your sanctuary,
for your love is better than life itself;
may our lips speak your praise,
our morning prayer glorify you
and our lives be spent in your service;
through Jesus Christ our Lord.

All:

Amen.

Psalm 15/16 (adapted): For You Are My God

Antiphon

John Foley, S.J.

For You are my God; You a - lone are my joy. De - fend me, O Lord.

Verses

1. You give mar - ve - lous com-rades to me: The faith - ful who dwell in Your land. Those who choose a - li - en gods have cho - sen an a - li - en band. *Antiphon*

2. You are my por - tion and cup; it is You that I claim for my prize. Your her - i - tage is my de - light, the lot you have giv - en to me. *Antiphon*

3. Glad are my heart and my soul; se-cure-ly my bo-dy shall rest. For you will not leave me for dead, nor lead your be-lov-ed a-stray. *Antiphon*

4. You show me the path for my life; in your pre-sence the full-ness of joy. To be at your right hand for-ev-er for me would be hap-pi-ness al-ways. *Antiphon*

Psalm Prayer

The leader invites everyone to pray in silence for a moment:
Let us pray.

Then the leader offers the following psalm prayer in the name of the community:
In your goodness, compassionate Father,
you reveal to us the path to new life.
May our words and works give you glory this day;
through Jesus Christ our Lord.

All:
Amen.

Psalm 91/92 (adapted): Like Cedars They Shall Stand

Antiphon

Dan Schutte, S.J.

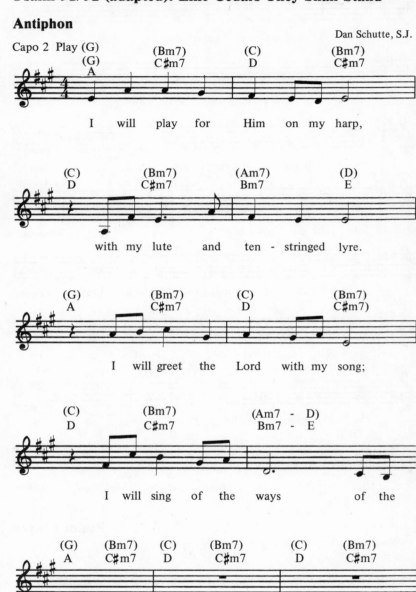

I will play for Him on my harp,
with my lute and ten - stringed lyre.
I will greet the Lord with my song;
I will sing of the ways of the
Lord.

(Am7 - G)	(D)		(G)	(Bm7)	(C)	(Bm7)
Bm7 - A	E		A	C#m7	D	C#m7

1.   Good it is that we should sing to
2.   Great and wide your kind-ness, Lord, and
3. Up - on my head you pour your oil; you
4. The just shall grow as tall as palms, like

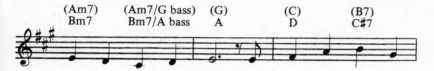

(Am7)	(Am7/G bass)	(G)	(C)	(B7)
Bm7	Bm7/A bass	A	D	C#7

1. hon - or Yah - weh's name, to thank him for His
2. fa - thoms deep your heart. The wick - ed man shall
3. mark me as your own And filled with glad - ness
4. ce - dars they shall stand. And plant - ed firm - ly

(Em)		(Am7)	(Am7/G)	(D)
F#m		Bm7	Bm7/A	E

1. love at dawn, his faith - ful - ness through the night.
2. not per - ceive; the fool - ish man shall fall.
3. I shall sing; my horn shall sound your call.
4. on their God, they shall not break nor bow.

Psalm Prayer

The leader invites everyone to pray in silence for a moment:
Let us pray.

Then the leader offers the following psalm prayer in the name of the community:
We proclaim your great love,
Lord our God,
as we begin this day.
May our lives be lived in your service.
This we ask through Jesus Christ our Lord.

All:
Amen.

Psalm 97/98 (adapted): Sing a New Song

Antiphon

Dan Schutte, S.J.

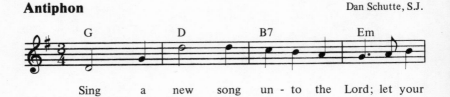

Sing a new song un - to the Lord; let your

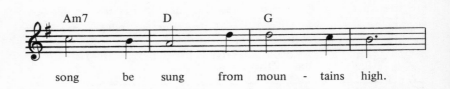

song be sung from moun - tains high.

Sing a new song un - to the Lord, sing-ing

al - le - lu - ia.

Verses

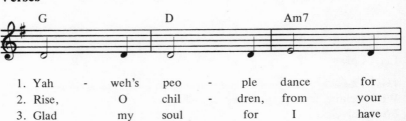

1. Yah - weh's peo - ple dance for
2. Rise, O chil - dren, from your
3. Glad my soul for I have

1. joy. O come be - fore the
2. sleep; your Sav - ior now has
3. seen the glo - ry of the

1. Lord. And play for Him on
2. come. He has turned your
3. Lord. The trum - pet sounds; the

1. glad tam - bou - rines, and let your
2. sor - row to joy, and filled your
3. dead shall be raised. I know my

1. trum - pet sound.
2. soul with song.
3. Sav - ior lives.

Psalm Prayer

The leader invites everyone to pray in silence for a moment:
Let us pray.

Then the leader offers the following psalm prayer in the name of the community:
Heavenly Father,
we sing your glory and shout out your goodness,
for you have called us to be your people.
May we always exult in your name.
This we pray through Jesus Christ our Lord.

All:
Amen.

THE WORD OF GOD Reading

All are seated *A brief Scripture passage is proclaimed by the reader:*

Understand this today, and take it to heart:
The Lord is God indeed, in heaven above as on earth beneath,
he and no other.
Keep his laws and commandments as I give them to you today,
so that you and your children may prosper and live long
in the land that the Lord your God gives you for ever. *(Deut. 4:39-40)*

At the end of the reading, the reader raises the Bible and says:

This is the word of the Lord.

All respond:

Thanks be to God.

All pray in silence, opening their minds and hearts to the Spirit.

Other brief readings:

Deuteronomy 6:4-7; 7:6	*Romans 12:9-13*
Isaiah 55:1-3	*Romans 12:14-21*
1 Thessalonians 5:2-10	*Romans 13:8-10*
2 Thessalonians 3:6-13	*Romans 13:11-13*
Romans 12:1-2	*2 Timothy 2:8, 11-13*

SONG OF PRAISE

All stand *A song of praise is prayed, either the Gloria or the Canticle of Zachary.*

Gloria in Excelsis

From "Congregational Mass — 1970"
John Lee, 1970

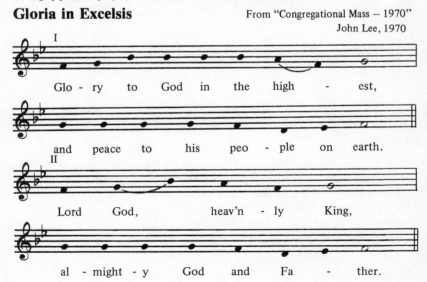

Glo - ry to God in the high - est,
and peace to his peo - ple on earth.
Lord God, heav'n - ly King,
al - might - y God and Fa - ther.

86

I
We wor - ship you, we give you thanks,

we praise you for your glo - ry.

II
Lord Je - sus Christ, on - ly Son of the Fa - ther,

Lord God, Lamb of God,

I
you take a - way the sin of the world: have mer - cy on us;

II
you are seat - ed at the right hand of the Fa - ther:

re - ceive our prayer.

I
For you a - lone are the Ho - ly One,

you a - lone are the Lord,

II
you a - lone are the Most High, Je - sus Christ,

with the Ho - ly Spir - it, *Slower*

in the glo - ry of God the Fa - ther. A - men.

87

Canticle of Zachary (Lk. 1:68-79)

Antiphons

Byzantine Chant
Arr. J.A.M.

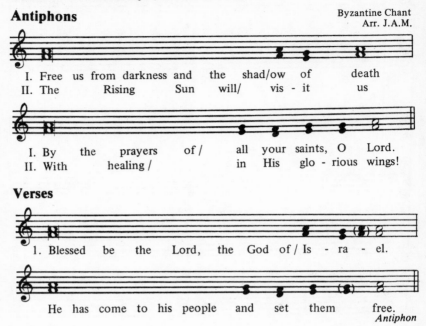

I. Free us from darkness and the shad/ow of death
II. The Rising Sun will/ vis - it us

I. By the prayers of / all your saints, O Lord.
II. With healing / in His glo - rious wings!

Verses

1. Blessed be the Lord, the God of / Is - ra - el.

He has come to his people and set them free.
Antiphon

2. He has raised up for us a / mighty savior,
   Born of the house of his / servant David.

3. Through his holy prophets he pro/mised of old
     that he would save us from our enemies,/
   From the hands of / all who hate us.

4. He promised to show mercy to / our fathers
   And to remember his / holy covenant.

5. This was the oath he swore to our father / Abraham:
   To Set us free from the hands / of our enemies,

6. Free to worship him / without fear,
   Holy and righteous in his sight all the / days of our life.

7. You, my child, shall be called the prophet of / the Most High;
   For you will go before the Lord / to prepare his way.

8. To give his people knowledge of / salvation
   By the forgive/ness of their sins.

9. In the tender compassion / of our God
   The dawn from on high shall / break upon us,

10. To shine on those who dwell in darkness
      and the shadow / of death,
    And to guide our feet in/to the way of peace.

11. Glory to the Father, and to the Son, and to
      the / Holy Spirit
    As it was in the beginning, is now, and will
      be for/ever. Amen.

Leader:

That we may walk in the light of Christ this day,
let us pray to the Lord.

All:

Lord, hear our prayer.

Leader:

That we may have a peaceful and prosperous day,
let us pray to the Lord.

All:

Lord, hear our prayer.

Leader:

That our work may be satisfying this day
and done for the glory and honor of God,
let us pray to the Lord.

All:

Lord, hear our prayer.

Other petitions for daily needs may be offered aloud or in silence.

Leader:

Lord our God,
you are loving and kind to your people,
accept our prayers this day,
and grant them as you see fit;
we offer them in the name of Jesus,
your Son and our Lord.

All:

Amen.

Leader:

With the Spirit crying in our hearts "Abba, Father," let us pray:

All:

Our Father...

Leader:

May Jesus Christ,
who has come for our salvation and who is coming again in glory,
guide and protect us this day.

All:

Amen.

THE LORD'S PRAYER

BLESSING

89

Morning Supplement

Psalm 62/63: Longing for God in the Shadow of the Cross

Antiphon *(Ordinary Time)*

H.H.

As morn - ing breaks I look to you, O God, to be my strength this day, al - le - lu - i - a.

Antiphon *(Lent)*

I will praise you all my life, O Lord; in your name I will lift up my hands.

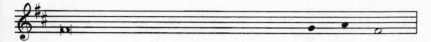

1. O God, you are my God, for you I long;
2. My body pines for you
3. So I gaze on you in the sanctuary
4. For your love is bet - ter than life,
5. So I will bless you all my life,
6. My soul shall be filled as with a banquet,
7. On my bed I remember you. On you I muse through the night
8. My soul clings to you;
9. Glory to the Father, and to the Son,
10. As it was in the be - ginning,

1. for you my soul is thirst - ing.
2. like a dry, weary land with - out wa - ter.
3. to see your strength and your glo - ry.
4. my lips will speak your praise.
5. in your name I will lift up my hands.
6. my mouth shall praise you with joy.
7. for you have been my help;/
   in the shadow of your wings I re - joice.
8. your right hand holds me fast.
9. and to the Ho - ly Spir - it.
10. is now and will be for ev - er. A - men.

Psalm Prayer

Leader:

Let us pray. *(Pause for silent prayer.)*

Father,
Source of unfailing light,
from early morning
we seek you in your sanctuary,
for your love is better than life itself.
As we lift our hands to you in prayer
and our hearts in songs of praise,
may our worship glorify you
and our lives be spent in your service;
through Jesus Christ our Lord.

All:

Amen.

Psalm 23/24: Jesus Is The King of Glory

Antiphon

H.H.

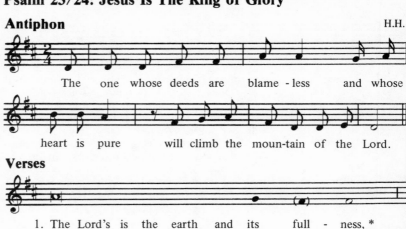

The one whose deeds are blame-less and whose heart is pure will climb the moun-tain of the Lord.

Verses

1. The Lord's is the earth and its full - ness, *
2. It is he who set it on the seas; *

1. the world and all its peo - ples.
2. on the waters he made it firm.

Antiphon

Who shall climb the mountain of the Lord? *
    Who shall stand in his holy place? - -
The man with clean hands and pure heart, / who desires not worthless things,*
    who has not sworn so as to deceive his neighbor.

Antiphon

He shall receive blessings from the Lord *
    and reward from the God who saves him.
Such are the men who seek him, * seek the face of the God of Jacob.

Antiphon

O gates, lift high your heads; / grow higher, ancient doors. *
    Let him enter, the king of glory!
Who is the king of glory? * The Lord, the mighty, the valiant, /
    the Lord, the valiant in war.

Antiphon

O gates, lift high your heads; / grow higher, ancient doors. *
    Let him enter, the king of glory!
Who is he, the king of glory? * He, the Lord of armies, / he is the king of glory.

Antiphon

Glory to the Father, and to the Son, and to the Holy Spirit.
As it was in the beginning, * is now and will be for ever. A-men.

Antiphon

Psalm Prayer

Leader:

Let us pray. *(Pause for silent prayer.)*

King of Glory, we your people seek your face.
Let your love touch our hearts this day.
May we enjoy your mercy, through Jesus Christ our Lord.

All:

Amen.

Psalm 92/93: Our Majestic Creator

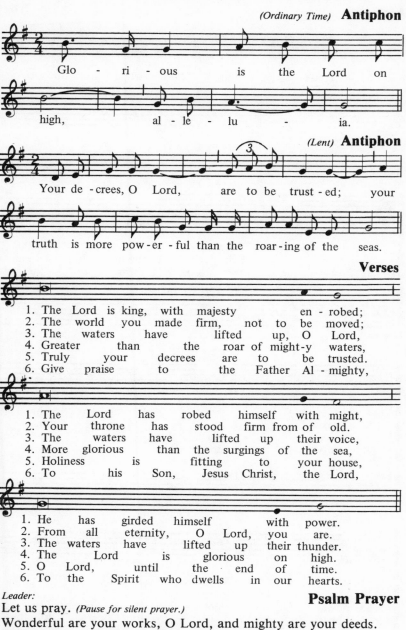

(Ordinary Time) **Antiphon**

Glo - ri - ous is the Lord on high, al - le - lu - ia.

(Lent) **Antiphon**

Your de - crees, O Lord, are to be trust - ed; your truth is more pow - er - ful than the roar - ing of the seas.

Verses

1. The Lord is king, with majesty en - robed;
2. The world you made firm, not to be moved;
3. The waters have lifted up, O Lord,
4. Greater than the roar of might-y waters,
5. Truly your decrees are to be trusted.
6. Give praise to the Father Al - mighty,

1. The Lord has robed himself with might,
2. Your throne has stood firm from of old.
3. The waters have lifted up their voice,
4. More glorious than the surgings of the sea,
5. Holiness is fitting to your house,
6. To his Son, Jesus Christ, the Lord,

1. He has girded himself with power.
2. From all eternity, O Lord, you are.
3. The waters have lifted up their thunder.
4. The Lord is glorious on high.
5. O Lord, until the end of time.
6. To the Spirit who dwells in our hearts.

Leader:

Psalm Prayer

Let us pray. *(Pause for silent prayer.)*

Wonderful are your works, O Lord, and mighty are your deeds.
We give you praise as we begin this day and we ask your mercy;
through Jesus Christ our Lord.

All:

Amen.

Psalm 112/113: Praise The Lord!

Antiphon

D.C.I.

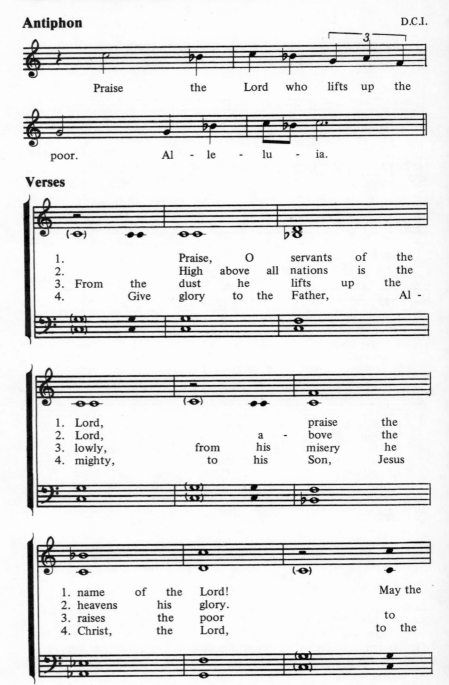

Praise the Lord who lifts up the poor. Al - le - lu - ia.

Verses

1. Praise, O servants of the Lord, praise the name of the Lord! May the
2. High above all nations is the Lord, a - bove the heavens his glory.
3. From the dust he lifts up the lowly, from his misery he raises the poor
4. Give glory to the Father, Al - mighty, to his Son, Jesus Christ, the Lord, to the

94

1. name of the Lord be blest
2. Who is like the Lord, our God,
3. set them in the company of princes,
4. Spirit who dwells in our hearts,

1. both now and for
2. who has risen on
3. yes, with the
4. both now and for

1. ever - more!
2. high to his throne?
3. princes of the people.
4. ever. A - men.

Psalm Prayer

Leader:

Let us pray. *(Pause for silent prayer.)*

Gracious God,
you cast down the mighty
and raise up the lowly.
Look with compassion on the downtrodden
and enable them to praise you,
through all the ages of ages.

All:

Amen.

Psalm 144/145: A Hymn of Praise

Antiphon

D.C.I.

The Lord is near to all who

call up - on him.

Verses

1. I will give you glory, O God my
2. I will bless you day after
3. Age to age shall pro - claim your
4. They will speak of your terri - ble
5. The Lord is kind and full of com -
6. All your creatures shall thank you, O
7. To make known to all your mighty

1. King,   [
2. day   and   praise   your
3. works,   shall de - clare   your
4. deeds,   re - count   your
5. passion,   slow   to   an - ger,   a -
6. Lord,   and   your   friends shall re -
7. deeds   and   the   glori - ous

1.
2. name   for   ever.   The Lord is
3. mighty   deeds,   shall
4. greatness   and   might.   They will re -
5. bounding   in   love.   How
6. peat   their   blessing.   They shall
7. splendour of your reign.

1.   ]
2. great,   highly   to   be   praised,
3. speak of your   splendour and   glory,
4. call   your   a - bundant   goodness;
5. good   is   the   Lord   to   all,
6. speak of   the   glory   of   your   reign
7. Yours   is   an   everlasting   kingdom;

1.   I will   bless   your   name   for   ever.
2.   his   greatness   cannot   be   measured.
3.   tell the   tale 'of your   wonderful   works.
4.   age to   age   shall   ring   out   your   justice.
5.   com - passionate to   all   his   creatures.
6.   and de - clare   your   might,   O   God,
7.   your   rule lasts from   age   to   age.

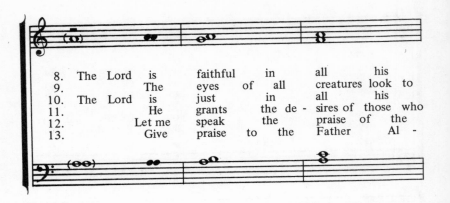

8. The Lord is   faithful   in   all   his
9.   The   eyes   of all   creatures look to
10. The Lord is   just   in   all   his
11.   He   grants   the de - sires of those who
12.   Let me speak   the   praise of the
13.   Give praise to the   Father   Al -

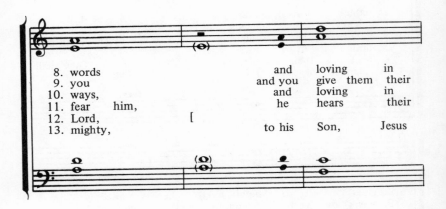

8. words   and   loving   in
9. you   and you give them their
10. ways,   and   loving   in
11. fear him,   he   hears   their
12. Lord,   [
13. mighty,   to his   Son,   Jesus

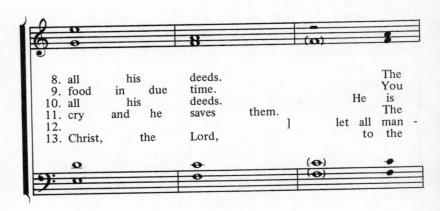

8. all   his   deeds.   The
9. food in due time.   You
10. all   his   deeds.   He is
11. cry and he   saves them.   The
12.   ]   let all man -
13. Christ, the   Lord,   to the

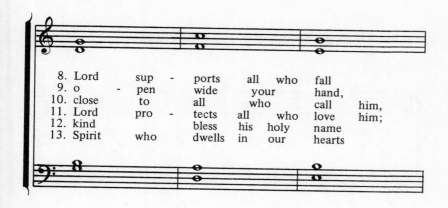

8. Lord sup - ports all who fall
9. o - pen wide your hand,
10. close to all who call him,
11. Lord pro - tects all who love him;
12. kind bless his holy name
13. Spirit who dwells in our hearts

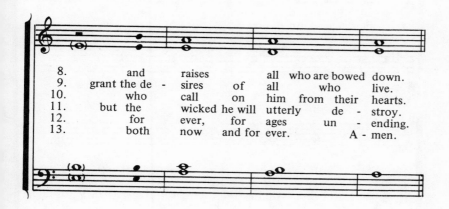

8. and raises all who are bowed down.
9. grant the de - sires of all who live.
10. who call on him from their hearts.
11. but the wicked he will utterly de - stroy.
12. for ever, for ages un - ending.
13. both now and for ever. A - men.

Psalm Prayer

Leader:
Let us pray. *(Pause for silent prayer.)*

Lord our God,
your name is praised from sunrise to sunset
because of your loving care for us.
Make us worthy to thank you for your great glory,
through Jesus Christ our Lord.

All:
Amen.

Psalm 145/146: Praise our Faithful God

Antiphon

D.C.I.

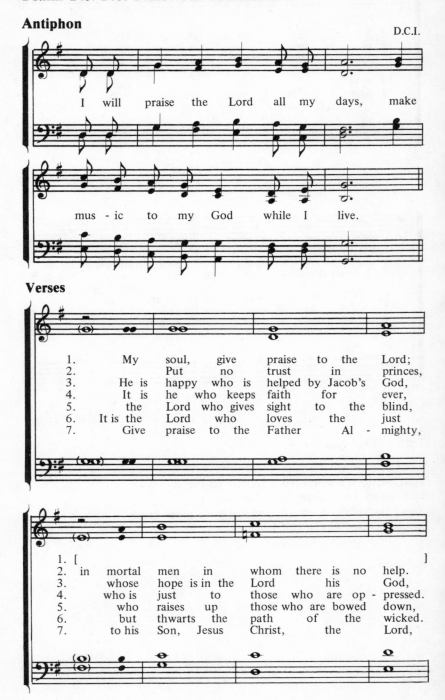

I will praise the Lord all my days, make

mus - ic to my God while I live.

Verses

1.	My	soul,	give	praise	to the	Lord;
2.		Put	no	trust	in	princes,
3.	He is	happy	who is	helped by	Jacob's	God,
4.	It is	he	who keeps	faith	for	ever,
5.	the	Lord	who gives	sight	to the	blind,
6.	It is the	Lord	who	loves	the	just
7.	Give	praise	to the	Father	Al -	mighty,

1. [						]
2.	in mortal	men	in	whom there	is	no help.
3.	whose	hope is in the	Lord	his		God,
4.	who is	just	to	those who	are op -	pressed.
5.	who	raises	up	those who	are bowed	down,
6.	but	thwarts the	path	of	the	wicked.
7.	to his	Son,	Jesus	Christ,	the	Lord,

100

1.	I will	praise	the	Lord	all my	days,
2.	Take their	breath,	they re-turn	to		clay
3.	who a -	lone	made	heaven	and	earth,
4.	It is	he who gives	bread	to	the	hungry,
5.	the	Lord, who pro-tects	the		stranger
6.	The	Lord	will	reign	for	ever,
7.	to the	Spirit	who	dwells	in our	hearts

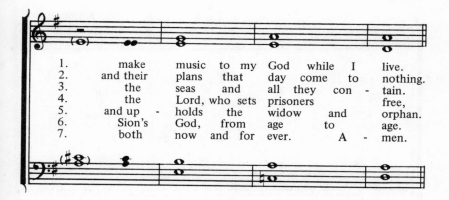

1.	make	music	to my	God	while I	live.
2.	and their	plans	that	day	come to	nothing.
3.	the	seas	and	all they	con -	tain.
4.	the	Lord, who sets	prisoners		free,
5.	and up -	holds	the	widow	and	orphan.
6.	Sion's	God,	from	age	to	age.
7.	both	now	and for	ever.	A -	men.

Psalm Prayer

Leader:

Let us pray. *(Pause for silent prayer.)*

You made us, O Lord,
and we belong to you;
we are yours both by nature and by grace;
with songs of praise and thanksgiving
we come into your presence with gladness and joy.
Blessed be your holy Name,
Father, Son and Holy Spirit,
now and always and for ever and ever.

All:

Amen.

Psalm 146/147a: Praise our Rescuing God

Antiphon

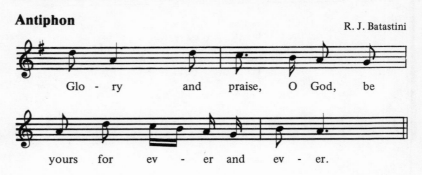

R. J. Batastini

Glo - ry and praise, O God, be

yours for ev - er and ev - er.

Verses

J. Gelineau, S.J.

1. Praise the Lord for he is
2. The Lord builds up Je -
3. Our Lord is great and
4. He covers the heavens with
5. His de - light is not in
6. Give praise to the Father Al -

1. good; sing to our God for
2. rusalem and brings back
3. mighty; his wisdom can
4. clouds; he pre - pares the
5. horses nor his pleasure in
6. mighty, to his Son, Jesus

1. he   is   loving: [
2. Is - ra - el's   exiles,   he   heals   the
3. nev - er be measured. The   Lord
4. rain for the earth, making moun - tains
5. war - ri - ors' strength. The Lord delights in
6. Christ, the Lord, to the Spirit who

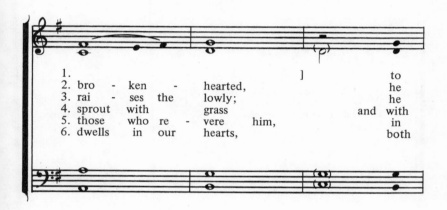

1.   ]   to
2. bro - ken - hearted,   he
3. rai - ses the lowly;   he
4. sprout with   grass   and with
5. those who re - vere him,   in
6. dwells in our hearts,   both

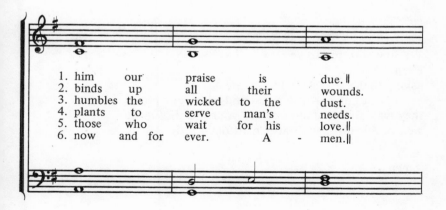

1. him   our   praise   is   due. ‖
2. binds up   all   their   wounds.
3. humbles the wicked to the dust.
4. plants to   serve   man's   needs.
5. those who   wait for his love. ‖
6. now and for ever.   A - men. ‖

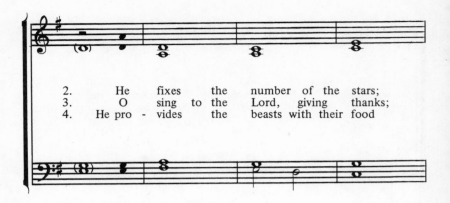

2.   He   fixes   the   number of the   stars;
3.   O   sing   to the   Lord,   giving   thanks;
4.   He pro - vides the   beasts with their food

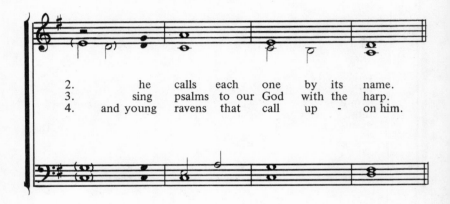

2.   he   calls   each   one   by its   name.
3.   sing   psalms to our God with the harp.
4.   and young ravens that call   up - on him.

Psalm Prayer

Leader:

Let us pray. *(Pause for silent prayer.)*

We sing with joy to you,
eternal Father,
asking that
as the gates of our hearts resound with your praise
they may always stand open to your merciful love;
we ask this through Jesus Christ our Lord.

All:
Amen.

Psalm 147b: Praise our Caring God

R. J. Batastini

Antiphon

Praise the Rul - er _____ of heav - en and earth!

J. Gelineau, S. J.

Verses

1. O praise the Lord, Je -
2. He has strengthened the bars of your
3. He sends out his word to the
4. He hurls down hailstones like
5. He makes his word known to
6. Give praise to the Father Al -

1. rusalem!   [
2. gates,   he has blessed the
3. earth   and swiftly
4. crumbs.   The waters are
5. Jacob,   to Israel his
6. mighty,   to his Son, Jesus

1.
2. children with - in you.   He es - tablished
3. runs his com - mand.   He showers down
4. frozen at his touch;   he sends forth his
5. laws and de - crees.   He has not dealt
6. Christ, the Lord,   to the Spirit who

105

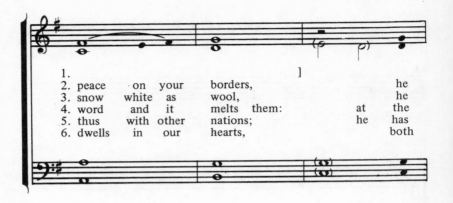

1.
2. peace on your borders,   he
3. snow white as wool,   he
4. word and it melts them: at the
5. thus with other nations;   he has
6. dwells in our hearts,   both

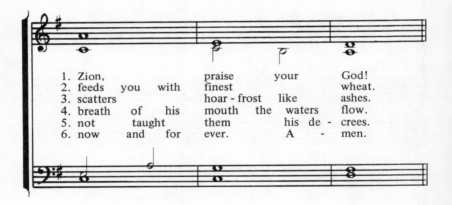

1. Zion,   praise your God!
2. feeds you with finest wheat.
3. scatters   hoar-frost like ashes.
4. breath of his mouth the waters flow.
5. not taught them   his de-crees.
6. now and for ever.   A - men.

Psalm Prayer

Leader:

Let us pray. *(Pause for silent prayer.)*

O God,
whose name is blessed from sunrise to sunset,
fill our hearts with knowledge of you
and make us worthy to sing your praise
and thank you for your great glory,
through Jesus Christ our Lord.

All:

Amen.

Psalm 148: Cosmic Praise

H.H.

Antiphon

Praise the Lord from the heav - ens, ___

al - le - lu - ia.

Verses

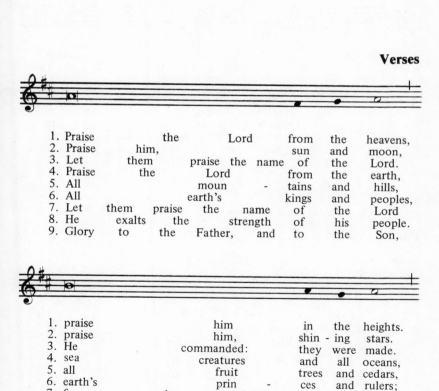

1. Praise the Lord from the heavens,
2. Praise him, sun and moon,
3. Let them praise the name of the Lord.
4. Praise the Lord from the earth,
5. All moun - tains and hills,
6. All earth's kings and peoples,
7. Let them praise the name of the Lord
8. He exalts the strength of his people.
9. Glory to the Father, and to the Son,

1. praise him in the heights.
2. praise him, shin - ing stars.
3. He commanded: they were made.
4. sea creatures and all oceans,
5. all fruit trees and cedars,
6. earth's prin - ces and rulers;
7. for he alone is ex - alted.
8. He is the praise of all his saints,
9. and to the Ho - ly Spirit.

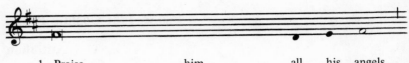

1. Praise		him,		all	his	angels,
2. Praise		him,		high - est	heavens
3. He		fixed		them	for	ever,
4. Fire	and		hail,	snow	and	mist,
5. Beasts,				wild	and	tame,
6. Young				men	and	maidens,
7. The		splendor		of	his	name
8. Of		the		sons	of	Israel,
9. As	it	was	in	the	be - ginning,

1. praise		him,			all	his	host.
2. and	the		waters	a - bove	the	heavens.
3. gave	a	law	which shall	not	pass	a - way.
4. stormy		winds	that	o - bey	his	word;
5. reptiles		and	birds	on	the	wing;
6. old		men	togeth	-	er	with children.
7. reaches		beyond	heav	-	en	and earth.
8. of	the	people	to	whom	he	comes close.
9. is	now	and	will	be for ev- er.	A - men.

Psalm Prayer

Leader:

Let us pray. *(Pause for silent prayer.)*

Almighty Lord,
who made firm the foundations of the universe,
make us trust in your decrees
and adorn us with holiness,
through Jesus Christ our Lord.

All:

Amen.

Psalm 149: Praise our Victorious God

R. J. Batastini

Antiphon

Sing a new song to the

God of sal - va - tion.

J. Gelineau, S.J.

Verses

1.   Sing a new song to the
2. For the Lord takes de - light in his
3.   to deal our vengeance to the
4. Give praise to the Father Al -

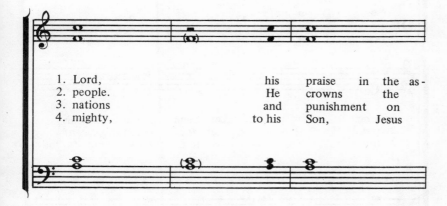

1. Lord,   his praise in the as -
2. people.   He crowns the
3. nations   and punishment on
4. mighty,   to his Son, Jesus

109

1. sembly of the faithful. Let
2. poor with sal - vation. Let the
3. all the peoples; to
4. Christ, the Lord, to the

1. Israel re - joice in its Maker,
2. faithful re - joice in their glory,
3. bind their kings in chains
4. Spirit who dwells in our hearts

1. let Zion's sons ex - ult in their
2. shout for joy and take their
3. and their nobles in fetters of
4. [

1. king. Let them praise his
2. rest. Let the praise of
3. iron; to carry out the
4.

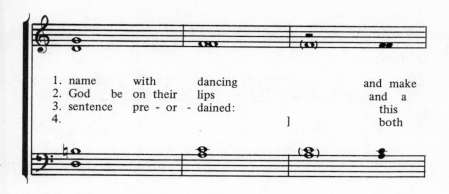

1. name with dancing and make
2. God be on their lips and a
3. sentence pre - or - dained: this
4.] both

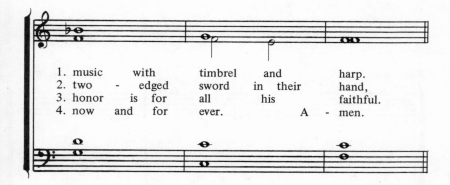

1. music with timbrel and harp.
2. two - edged sword in their hand,
3. honor is for all his faithful.
4. now and for ever. A - men.

Psalm Prayer

Leader:

Let us pray. *(Pause for silent prayer.)*

O God,
the Author of peace and Lover of concord,
to know you is to live,
to serve you is to reign;
defend us from all the assaults of our enemies,
that we who trust in your protection
may have no foe to fear;
through the power of Jesus Christ our Lord.

All:

Amen.

Canticle of David (1 Chron. 29:10-13)

Antiphon

R. J. Batastini

Yours, O Lord, are gran - deur and strength; we

praise and ex - alt your name.

Verses

J. Gelineau, S.J.

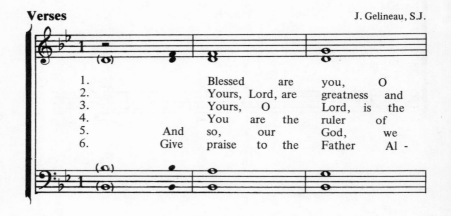

1. Blessed are you, O
2. Yours, Lord, are greatness and
3. Yours, O Lord, is the
4. You are the ruler of
5. And so, our God, we
6. Give praise to the Father Al -

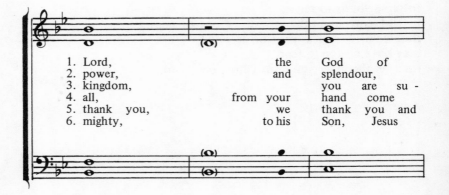

1. Lord, the God of
2. power, and splendour,
3. kingdom, you are su -
4. all, from your hand come
5. thank you, we thank you and
6. mighty, to his Son, Jesus

112

1. Israel our father, for
2. triumph and glory. All is
3. preme over all. Both
4. strength and power, from your
5. praise your name, we
6. Christ, the Lord, to the

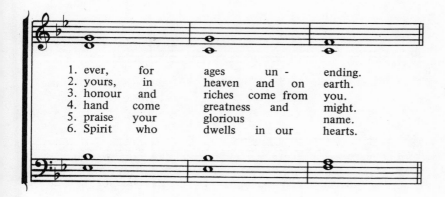

1. ever, for ages un - ending.
2. yours, in heaven and on earth.
3. honour and riches come from you.
4. hand come greatness and might.
5. praise your glorious name.
6. Spirit who dwells in our hearts.

Prayer

Leader:

Let us pray. *(Pause for silent prayer.)*

God of Abraham, Isaac and Jacob,
Father of our Lord Jesus Christ,
everything we have comes from you,
all is yours.
Watch over your chosen people,
shape their lives by your law,
and direct their hearts to you.
We ask this through Christ our Lord.

All:

Amen.

Canticle of the Three Children (Dan 3:52-56)

Book of Common Prayer, 1977
Tone VIIIa

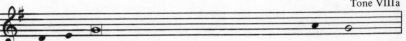

1. Glo - ry to you, Lord God of our fa - thers;

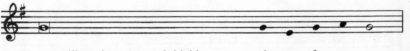

you are worthy of praise; glo - ry to you.

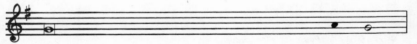

2. Glory to you for the radiance of your holy Name;

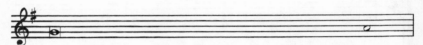

we will praise you and highly ex - alt you for ev - er.

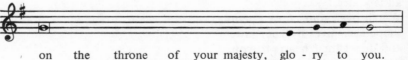

3. Glory to you in the splendor of your tem - ple;

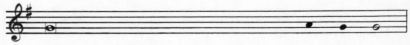

on the throne of your majesty, glo - ry to you.

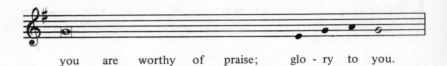

4. Glory to you, seated between the Cher - u - bim;

114

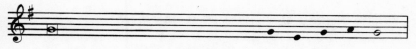

we will praise you and highly ex - alt you for ev - er.

5. Glory to you, beholding the depths;

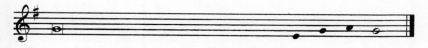

in the high vault of heaven, glo - ry to you.

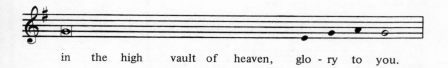

6. Glory to you, Father, Son, and Holy Spir - it;

we will praise you and highly exalt you for ev - er.

Prayer

Leader:

Let us pray. *(Pause for silent prayer.)*

Lord Jesus Christ,
by your death and resurrection,
you reconciled everything in heaven and on earth.
By the power of your passion,
set us apart to sing the praise of God
in union with all the saints and angels,
now and for ever.

All:

Amen.

Canticle of the Three Children (Dan 3:57-87)

One or more sections of this Canticle may be used. Whatever the selection, it begins with the Invocation and concludes with the Doxology.

Invocation

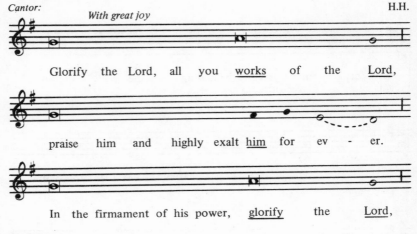

Cantor: With great joy   H.H.

Glorify the Lord, all you works of the Lord,

praise him and highly exalt him for ev - er.

In the firmament of his power, glorify the Lord,

Refrain

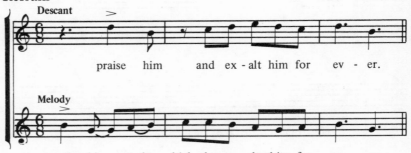

Descant

praise him and ex - alt him for ev - er.

Melody

praise him_ and _ high - ly ex - alt him for ev - er.

Verses

I   The Cosmic Order

1. Glorify the Lord, you angels and all powers of the Lord, *
   O heavens and all waters above the heavens.
   Sun and moon and stars of the sky, glorify the Lord, *
   praise him and highly exalt him for ever.

2. Glorify the Lord, every shower of rain and fall of dew, *
   all winds and fire and heat.
   Winter and summer, glorify the Lord, *
   praise him and highly exalt him for ever.

3. Glorify the Lord, O chill and cold, *
   drops of dew and flakes of snow.
   Frost and cold, ice and sleet, glorify the Lord, *
   praise him and highly exalt him for ever.

116

4. Glorify the Lord, O nights and days, *
    O shining light and enfolding dark.
  Storm clouds and thunderbolts, glorify the Lord, *
    praise him and highly exalt him for ever.

II   The Earth and its Creatures

5. Let the earth glorify the Lord, *
    praise him and highly exalt him for ever.
  Glorify the Lord, O mountains and hills, /
  and all that grows upon the earth, *
    praise him and highly exalt him for ever.

6. Glorify the Lord, O springs of water, seas, and streams, *
    O whales and all that move in the waters.
  All birds of the air, glorify the Lord, *
    praise him and highly exalt him for ever.

7. Glorify the Lord, O beasts of the wild, *
    and all you flocks and herds.
  O men and women everywhere, glorify the Lord, *
    praise him and highly exalt him for ever.

III   The People of God

8. Let the people of God glorify the Lord, *
    praise him and highly exalt him for ever.
  Glorify the Lord, O priests and servants of the Lord, *
    praise him and highly exalt him for ever.

9. Glorify the Lord, O spirits and souls of the righteous,
    praise him and highly exalt him for ever.
  You that are holy and humble of heart, glorify the Lord, *
    praise him and highly exalt him for ever.

Doxology

Let us glorify the Lord: Father, Son, and Holy Spirit; *
  praise him and highly exalt him for ever.
In the firmament of his power, glorify the Lord, *
  praise him and highly exalt him for ever.

Prayer

Leader:

Let us pray. *(Pause for silent prayer.)*

Lord Jesus Christ,
you descended with the glory of the Father
into the midst of the fiery furnace
and delivered the three young men
from the hands of the Chaldeans.
Enlighten our minds with the radiance of your Gospel,
make us worthy to keep your commandments
and confer upon us the crown of light and life
promised to those who love you.
You live and reign now and for ever.

All:

Amen.

Canticle of Zachary (Lk. 1:67-79)

Antiphon

D.C.I.

The Son of right - eous - ness will a -

rise with heal - ing in his wings.

Verses

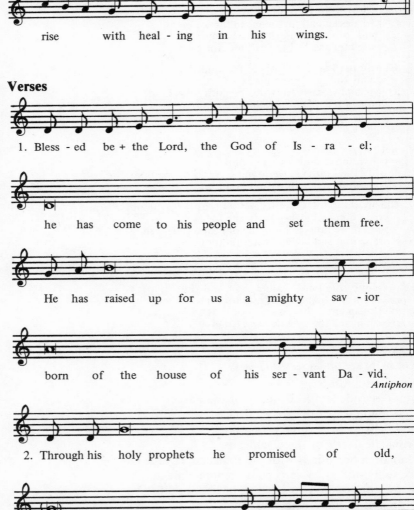

1. Bless - ed be + the Lord, the God of Is - ra - el;

he has come to his people and set them free.

He has raised up for us a mighty sav - ior

born of the house of his ser - vant Da - vid.
Antiphon

2. Through his holy prophets he promised of old,

that he would save us from our en - e - mies

118

from the hands of all who hate us.

He promised to show mercy to our fa - thers,

and to remember his ho - ly cov - e - nant.

Antiphon

3. This was the oath he swore to our father A - bra - ham:

to set us free from the hands of our en - e - mies.

Free to worship him without fear, holy and

righteous in his sight all the days of our lives.

Antiphon

4. You, my child, shall be called the prophet of the Most High;

for you will go before the Lord to pre - pare his way,

to give his people knowledge of sal - va - tion

by the for - give - ness of their sins.

Antiphon

5. In the tender compassion of our God the dawn from on high

shall break up - on us, to shine

on those who dwell in darkness and the shad - ow of death,

and to guide our feet into the way of peace.

Antiphon

6. Glo - ry to the Father, and to the Son,

and to the Holy Spir - it:

as it was in the beginning

is now, and will be for ev - er. A - men.

Antiphon

120

Canticle of Zachary (Lk. 1:67-79)

H.H.
Trans., James Quinn, S.J., 1975

Antiphon

The ris - ing Sun will vis - it us — — with heal - ing in his wings.

Verses

1. Bless'd be + the God of Israel The ever-living Lord,
2. Through holy prophets did he speak His words in days of old,
3. Of old he gave his solemn oath To father Abraham;
4. O tiny child, your name shall be The prophet of the Lord;
5. The rising sun shall shine on us To bring the light of day

1. Who comes in pow'r to save his own His people Israel.
2. That he would save us from our foes And all who bear us ill.
3. His seed a mighty race should be And bless'd for ever - more.
4. The way of God you shall pre-pare To make his coming known.
5. To all who sit in darkest night And shadow of the grave.

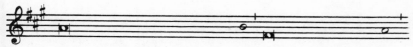

1. For Israel he raises up Salvation's tow'r on high
2. To our ancestors did he give His covenant of love;
3. He vowed to set his people free From fear of ev'ry foe,
4. You shall proclaim to Israel Salvation's dawning day,
5. Our footsteps God shall safely guide To walk the ways of peace.

1. In David's house who reigned as king And servant of the Lord.
2. So with us all he keeps his word In love that knows no end.
3. That we might serve him all our days In goodness, love and peace.
4. When God shall wipe away our sins In his redeeming love.
5. His name for evermore be bless'd Who lives and loves and saves.

121

Canticle of Zachary (Lk. 1:67-79)

M.J.
Trans., James Quinn, S.J., 1975

Antiphon

The ris - ing sun will vis - it us with
heal - ing in his glo - rious wings.

Verses

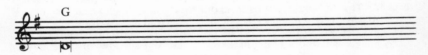

1. Blessed be + the Lord, the
2. Through his holy prophets he promised of old, that he would save us
3. This was the was the oath he swore to our
4. You, my child, shall be called the prophet of
5. In the tender compassion
6. Glory to the Father, and

1. God of Israel;
2. from our enemies,
3. fa - ther Abraham:
4. the Most High
5. of our God
6. to the Son,

122

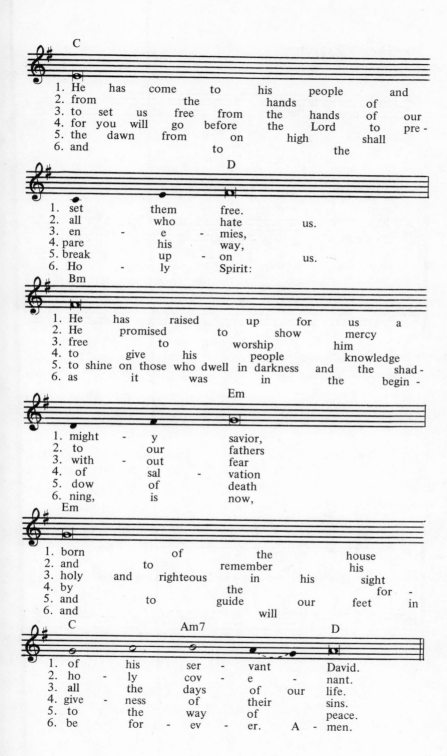

C

1. He has come to his people and
2. from the hands of
3. to set us free from the hands of our
4. for you will go before the Lord to pre -
5. the dawn from on high shall
6. and to the

D

1. set them free.
2. all who hate us.
3. en - e - mies,
4. pare his way,
5. break up - on us.
6. Ho - ly Spirit:

Bm

1. He has raised up for us a
2. He promised to show mercy
3. free to worship him
4. to give his people knowledge
5. to shine on those who dwell in darkness and the shad -
6. as it was in the begin -

Em

1. might - y savior,
2. to our fathers
3. with - out fear
4. of sal - vation
5. dow of death
6. ning, is now,

Em

1. born of the house
2. and to remember his
3. holy and righteous in his sight
4. by the for -
5. and to guide our feet in
6. and will

C   **Am7**   **D**

1. of his ser - vant David.
2. ho - ly cov - e - nant.
3. all the days of our life.
4. give - ness of their sins.
5. to the way of peace.
6. be for - ev - er. A - men.

123

The Lord's Prayer

H.H.

Our Fa - ther, who art in heav - en,

Our Fa - ther, who art in heav - en,

hal - lowed be thy name; thy king - dom come; thy

hal - lowed be thy name; thy king - dom come; thy

124

will be done on earth as it is in heav - en.

will be done on earth as it is in heav - en.

Give us this day our dai - ly bread; and for -

Give us this day our dai - ly bread; and for -

give us our tres - pas - ses, as we for -

give us our tres - pas - ses, as we for -

give those who tres - pass a - gainst us; and

give those who tres - pass a - gainst us; and

lead us not in - to temp - ta - tion, but de -

lead us not in - to temp - ta - tion, but de -

liv - er us from e - vil.

liv - er us from e - vil.

For the king-dom, the pow'r, and the glo-ry are

For the king-dom, the pow'r, and the glo-ry are

For the king-dom, the pow'r, and the glo-ry are

yours, now and for ev - er!

yours, now and for ev - er!

yours, now and for ev - er!

The Lord's Prayer

D.C.I.

Our Fa - ther, who art in heav - en,

hal - low - ed be thy name; thy king - dom come; thy

will be done on earth as it is in heav'n. Give

us this day our dai - ly bread and for -

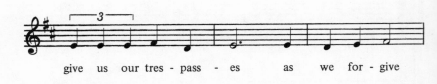

give us our tres - pass - es as we for - give

those ____ who tres - pass a - gainst us; and

128

lead   us   not   in - to   temp - ta - tion,   but de -

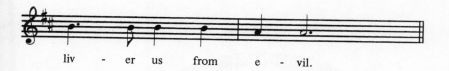

liv   -   er   us   from   e   -   vil.

For   the   king - dom and   the __ pow - er,   and the

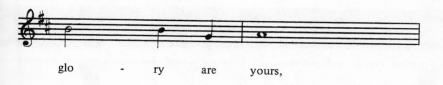

glo   -   ry   are   yours,

now   and   for - ev - er   A   -   men.

now   and   for - ev - er   A   -   men.

now   and   for - ev - er   A   -   men.

Evening Prayer

Evening Prayer

Light

The introductory *lucernarium* (Lat. *lucerna* = lamp) springs from the ancient practice of the churches of beginning evening prayer with the lighting of lamps to provide light for the service. In the famous Church of the Holy Sepulcher at Jerusalem, for example, the IV century pilgrim Egeria tells us: "At four o'clock they have *Lychnicon*, as they call it, or in our language, *Lucernare* [lamplighting]. All the people congregate once more in the Anastasis [the courtyard in front of the tomb], and the lamps and candles are all lit, which makes it very bright." (24:4) Perhaps in this age of the incandescent bulb and the fluorescent tube it is difficult for us to appreciate the wonder of flickering oil lamps piercing the settling darkness of the night, but pre-Edison cultures greeted artificial light each evening with grateful welcome. Pre-Christian Greeks had a custom of crying out "O goodly light!" when a lamp was brought into a darkening room and the lighting of the great golden menorah in the Temple each evening was one of the key ritual moments of the day (Exodus 25:31-40; Lev. 24:1-4) which influenced later synagogue liturgies and possibly the early Christian churches.

Our *lucernarium* rejoices in Jesus Christ, the light of the world, and expresses thanks for his radiating presence in our lives. The hymn *(Phos Hilaron)* is a text of the II/III century, traditional in Eastern churches at Vespers and is now used in the Office of Taize, the English *Book of Common Prayer* (1970), the American Episcopal *Book of Common Prayer* (1977) and is recommended in the Roman General Instruction on the Liturgy of the Hours (1971). On occasion hymns of the same theme may be substituted for the *Phos Hilaron*, especially during the strong seasons of Advent-Christmastide and Lent-Easter.

In a larger setting, the ministers may enter in procession: a thurifer with a burning censer, an assistant minister carrying a large, lighted candle, a reader with the Scriptures, cantor and leader. The procession may halt in the middle of the church for the Light Proclamation and then proceed as the Light Hymn is sung.

On more festive evenings, other lamps and candles may be lit from the central candle; on occasion, light may be distributed throughout the congregation. During Advent, an advent wreath may be the focus of the *lucernarium;* during Eastertide, the paschal candle.

The assistant proclaims the Evening Thanksgiving *(eucharistia lucernaris)* at the lectern. Alternative forms for ordinary time and for the special seasons may be found in the Evening Supplement.

Incense

Psalm 140/141 is the evening psalm *par excellence* and the original nucleus of Vespers in all liturgical families. By it we pray for the forgiveness of our faults and failings of the past day and ask to be saved from all sin during the on-coming evening and throughout the night. This "psalm at the kindling of the lamps" (*Apost. Const.* II, 59; VIII, 35) is traditionally used with incense considered either as an atonement symbol (Num. 16) or as a symbol of intercessory prayer (Rev. 8:3-4) and is a kind of rejuvenation of Temple usages (Exod. 30:1-10; 34-38; 37:25-29) connected with the daily holocausts and the trimming of the lamps at dawn and dusk. For Christians, Psalm 140/141:2 recalls the outstretched arms of Jesus on the cross in the evening of his life and "the sweet odor of Jesus Christ" (2 Cor. 2:14-16) which saturates the lives of those who receive him as their Lord and Savior. Incense can be an expressive reminder of the Lamb who was slain for our salvation, who "gave himself up in our place as a fragrant offering and sacrifice to God" (Eph. 5:2) and "who lives forever to plead with God" on our behalf (Heb. 7:25).

When incense is used, it may be burned in a stable brazier standing before the Lord's table or in the midst of the congregation or it may be burned in a portable censer (thurible). In the latter case the leader fills the censer and the assistant incenses everyone present as fully as time permits. When one is incensed, one may take the smoke in one's hands (as it were) and make the sign of the cross. In Eastern churches this form of purification-incensation is looked upon as a kind of non-verbal absolution.

Psalmody

Other psalms, canticles or hymns may be added to Psalm 140/141. In the parochial tradition these are few in number and chosen for their relevance to evening prayer. Psalm 120/121 and a few other songs found in the Evening Prayer Supplement are provided by way of example. On the eve of the greater festivals, appropriate festal psalms could be used at this point. In choral celebrations, the choir might sing an anthem either here or after the Scripture reading.

Whatever the selection of songs or the mode of execution, it is important to remember that the indicated pauses after the psalms and canticles are essential, not accessory, to their performance. These meditative pauses should be jealously guarded against erosion so that the sequence, psalm-pause-prayer, remains a liturgical unit helpful to personal prayer.

Either kneeling or sitting seems appropriate for the pauses; standing is suggested during the psalm prayers, especially in larger groups.

The evening psalmody may be concluded by Psalm 116/117 with the *Trisagion* as its refrain or by some other doxology, e.g., "Praise God from Whom All Blessings Flow."

The Word of God

The reader goes to the lectern to proclaim the Word of God, even when it is only a brief selection.

If longer readings are desired, they may be found in the Table of Longer Readings in the Appendix or in another standard lectionary (Anglican, Lutheran, Taizé). Some groups will perfer to read a book of the Bible in course, according to the sense divisions found in all modern bibles.

On the eve of special celebrations, additional readings (biblical, patristic, modern) and a brief homily may be appropriate. At all times silent reflection should follow each reading.

Canticle of Praise

In company with Psalm 140/141, a Gospel Canticle (East: Simeon; West: Mary) is one of the most ancient components of evening prayer. With the Canticle of Zachary (morning), they are the New Testament songs of praise *par excellence* and a fitting climax to the praise portion of the hours of prayer. The Canticle of Mary is especially appropriate for Saturdays, Sundays and festivals and is often used with incense to symbolize our participation in the Communion of Saints (Rev. 8:3-4). The Song of Simeon may be used on ordinary weekdays, especially when Vespers is held somewhat later in the evening.

The Gospel Canticles are sung standing and all sign themselves with the sign of the cross as they are begun. They "should be accorded the same solemnity and dignity as is usual for the hearing of the Gospel." (GILH, 138)

Petitions

From the very beginning, Christians have included general intercession for the Church and the world as a fundamental part of their communal and private prayer. "I urge that petitions, prayers, requests, and thanksgivings be offered to God for all people....This is good and it pleases God our Savior, who wants everyone to be saved and to come to know the truth." (1 Tim. 2:1, 3) Early on, the litany style of petitionary prayer became its normal pattern in most churches and leading the litany was considered a diaconal function.

On solemn occasions, many Christians will find useful the Roman Litany of the Saints, the Anglican Great Litany (BCP, 1979), the Roman General Intercessions for Good Friday or the Solemn Collects (BCP, 1979). The new Anglican, Roman, Lutheran and Taizé books contain several other sets of intercessory prayer which may be adapted to Office use. Many Roman Catholics will be comfortable with one of the devotional litanies from the old *Manual of Prayers* (Holy Name,

Sacred Heart, Holy Spirit, BVM, St. Joseph).

The time for Free Prayer should not be unduly prolonged nor used simply to repeat what has already been prayed for in the Litany. Each petition should be followed by a brief silence.

The Concluding Prayer may be one of those set forth in the text or the prayer of the day.

Except on the Lord's Day and during Eastertide, kneeling is customary during intercessory prayer.

The Lord's Prayer

To conclude our evening worship, it is only fitting to employ the Lord's own prayer, "a summary of the entire Gospel" (Tertullian). In its every phrase it speaks of the coming reign of God and, above all, it asks in faith for the forgiveness of sins and the reconciliation of the praying community. St. Benedict of Nursia wanted it prayed aloud each day at the conclusion of Lauds and Vespers: "Since the thorns of scandal are likely to arise in monasteries, the recitation of this prayer affords the monks an opportunity to cleanse themselves from this sort of vice through the mutual covenant they make in the words: 'Forgive us as we forgive'." (*Rule*, 13)

Closing

Finally, a trinitarian Blessing is invoked upon the community and a Sign of Peace seals this liturgy of Christian fellowship.

Evening Prayer

MUSICAL SETTING: DAVID CLARK ISELE

The church or room is dimly lit as the service begins.

LIGHT Light Proclamation

All stand *The assistant stands before the candle and sings:*

Light and peace in Je sus Christ our Lord.

All respond:

Thanks be to God.

The electric lights may be turned up if needed.

O Radiant Light
Trans., W.G.S.

1. O ra-diant Light, O Sun di-vine, of God the
2. O Son of God, the Source of life, praise is your
3. Lord Je-sus Christ, as day-light fades, as shine the

1. Fa-ther's death-less face, O im-age of the Light sub-
2. due by night and day. Our hap-py lips must raise the
3. lights of e-ven-tide, We praise the Fa-ther with the

1. lime that fills the heav'n-ly dwell-ing place.
2. strain of your es-teemed and splen-did name.
3. Son, the Spir-it blest and with them one.

Evening Thanksgiving

Assistant:

Let   us   give   thanks to

God   the Fa - ther   al - ways and for ev - 'ry -

All:

thing.   In   the   name   of   our   Lord Je - sus Christ.

Assistant:

Praised   be   the   Lord   our   God ,   Rul - er   of   the

un - i - verse, who   led   our   an - ces-tors   in the faith   by a

pil - lar   of cloud by   day,   and   a   pil - lar   of fire   by

night,   and   pre - pared   a   lamp for his   A   noint - ed.

138

Light up our dark-ness, O God, by the light of your Christ; may his word be a lamp to our feet and a light to our path, for you are full of lov - ing kind-ness for your whole cre - a - tion and we, your crea-tures, glo - ri - fy you, Fa - ther, Son and Ho - ly Spir - it. Now and for

All:

ev - er. A - men.

INCENSE Psalm 140/141: Evening Prayer for Forgiveness and Protection

The psalms in this service are sung in a responsorial manner, i.e., the cantor sings the antiphon and all repeat it; then the cantor sings the verses of the psalm and all repeat the antiphon as indicated. Some form of incensation may accompany the singing of this psalm.

Assistant:

Let us pray for par - don and for peace and for pro - tec - tion through-out the com - ing night.

Antiphon

My prayers rise like in - cense, my hands like an eve - ning off' - ring.

Verses

1. I call to you, Lord, help me now. Lis - ten to me when I call to you. Lord, I say to you, hear me. Lis - ten to me, Lord, I am in - vok - ing you.

Antiphon

140

2. Lord, place a guard ov-er my mouth, a sen-try at the door of my lips, keep my heart from in-clin-ing to e-vil. Save me from all wick-ed deeds and de-sires. Lis-ten to me, Lord, I am in-vok-ing you.

Antiphon

3. May the right-eous re-prove me in kind-ness, but I will not let the wick-ed a-noint my head. I will al-ways re-sist their e-vil deeds. Lis-ten to me, Lord, I am in-vok-ing you.

Antiphon

4. Lord God, my eyes are turned to you, defend and pro-tect me, in you I take re-fuge.

Guard me from the traps they have set for me,

from the snare of those who do ev-il.

Lis-ten to me, Lord, I am in-vok-ing you.

Antiphon

5. Glo-ry to the Fa-ther and to the Son, and
to the Ho-ly Spir-it as it
was in the be-gin-ning, is now and will be for-
ev-er. Lis-ten to me, Lord,

142   I am in-vok-ing you.

Antiphon

Psalm Prayer

The leader invites all to pray in silence for a moment:
Let us pray.

Then the leader offers one of the following prayers in the name of the community:

Sunday
Father of glory,
you raised our Lord Jesus Christ from the dead
and made him sit at your right hand in heaven.
Rescue us from our sins,
bring us to new life in Him
and give us a place in heaven,
with the same Christ Jesus our Lord.

All:
Amen.

Friday
Almighty and everlasting God,
may our prayers rise like incense before you,
our hands like an evening sacrifice.
As we contemplate your presence in word and sacrament
and in the lives of those around us,
stir up in us the flame of that love
which Jesus kindled on earth by his passion
and which burns in our hearts by the Holy Spirit.
You are one God for ever and ever.

All:
Amen.

Weekdays
Look down, O Lord, from your heavenly throne,
and illumine the darkness of this coming night
with your celestial brightness;
from the children of light
banish the deeds of darkness,
through Jesus Christ our Lord.

All:
Amen.

Advent

To you, Lord God, our eyes are turned
as we stand in eager expectation
of that day when peace shall flow from Zion
and the deserts shall bloom with your justice.
As our prayers ascend to you like the fragrance of incense
may your glory come down upon us
in the kingdom of your Son
who will live and reign with you and the Holy Spirit,
for ever and ever.

All:
Amen.

Christmas

Lord of glory and Creator of all,
you anointed Jesus with your favor.
He has dwelt among us and become our offering.
Accept the gift of incense,
our prayer which rises before you.
Shed Christ's light upon the darkness of our hearts
and free us from all that is evil.
We ask this in the name of Jesus the Christ
who with the Holy Spirit and you
is worthy of all glory,
now and for ever.

All:
Amen.

144

Lent

Lord God, our Father,
in this season of repentance
we beg you to receive our sacrifice of praise.
Throughout these forty days
may our voices cry to you in unceasing prayer,
our bodies abstain from the feasts of the wicked
and our hearts be turned to the needs of your people.
We ask this through Christ our Lord.

All:
Amen.

Easter

O God, our Father and Liberator,
Jesus Christ, your Son and our brother,
turned his eyes to you even in death.
You spared his soul
and anointed his head with glory.
May our prayers rise before you like incense
and our evening be the favored moment
of your peace and spirit,
in Jesus our risen Lord.

All:
Amen.

PSALMODY Psalm 120/121: We Are a Pilgrim People

All are seated *Psalm 120/121, some other evening psalm or a New Testament Canticle may be sung at this point.*

Antiphon

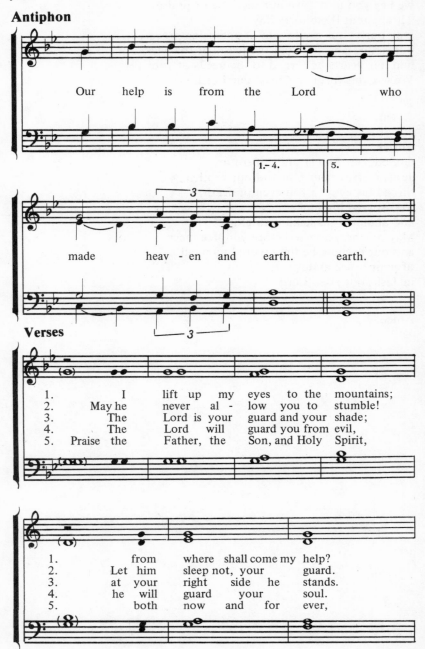

Our help is from the Lord who made heav - en and earth. earth.

Verses

1.   I   lift up   my   eyes to the   mountains;
2. May he   never al -   low you to   stumble!
3.   The   Lord is your   guard and your   shade;
4.   The   Lord will   guard you from evil,
5. Praise the   Father, the   Son, and Holy   Spirit,

1.   from   where shall come my help?
2. Let him   sleep not, your   guard.
3. at your   right side he   stands.
4. he will   guard your   soul.
5.   both   now and for   ever,

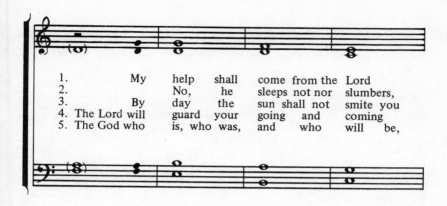

1. My help shall come from the Lord
2. No, he sleeps not nor slumbers,
3. By day the sun shall not smite you
4. The Lord will guard your going and coming
5. The God who is, who was, and who will be,

1. who made heaven and earth.
2. Israel's guard.
3. nor the moon in the night.
4. both now and for - ever.
5. world without end

Psalm Prayer

Leader invites everyone to pray in silence for a moment:
Let us pray.

Then the leader offers the following psalm prayer in the name of the community:
Lord Jesus Christ,
you have prepared a place for us
in your Father's eternal home.
Watch over our welfare on this perilous journey,
guard us from life's dangers,
and keep our lives free from evil until the end.
Yours is the power and the glory for ever and ever.

All:
Amen.

All stand **Psalm 116/117: A Doxology**

The evening psalmody may be concluded with Psalm 116/117 or some other doxology.

Assistant:

Let us lift up our voic-es and glo-ri-fy the liv-ing God.

Antiphon I

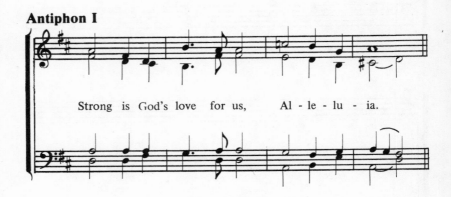

Strong is God's love for us, Al-le-lu-ia.

Antiphon II

Ho-ly is God, Ho-ly and strong,

Ho-ly and liv-ing for-ev-er!

148

O praise the Lord, all you na-tions, ac-claim him all you

peo - ples! Strong is his love for us; he is

faith - ful for - ev - er.

Antiphon

149

Glo - ry to the Fa - ther, and to the

Son, and to the Ho - ly Spir - it, for

ev - er and ev - er. A - men.

Antiphon

There is no psalm prayer after this psalm.

A reader proclaims the word of God:
Brothers and sisters,
I beg you through the mercy of God
to offer your bodies as a living sacrifice
holy and acceptable to God, your spiritual worship.
Do not conform yourselves to this age
but be transformed by the renewal of your mind,
so that you may judge what is God's will,
what is good, pleasing and perfect. *(Romans 12:1-2)*

At the end of the reading, the reader raises the Bible and says:
This is the word of the Lord.

All respond:
Thanks be to God.

After the reading, all pray in silence, opening their minds and hearts to the Spirit.

Other brief readings:

Romans 5:6-11
1 Corinthians 9:24-27
Galatians 6:7-10
Ephesians 6:10-18
Philippians 4:4-9
Colossians 3:12-17
Titus 2:11-14
1 Timothy 6:12-16
Hebrews 12:1-2
1 Peter 5:6-11
1 John 4:7-12
Revelation 22:1-5

CANTICLE
OF PRAISE Canticle of Mary (Lk. 1:46-55)

All stand *During this song, the altar and the community may be honored with incense. All make a sign of the cross as the canticle begins:*

Trans., J. T. Mueller, 1940, alt.

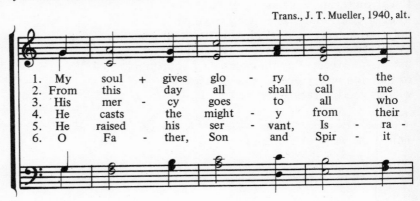

1. My soul + gives glo - ry to the
2. From this day all shall call me
3. His mer - cy goes to all who
4. He casts the might - y from their
5. He raised his ser - vant, Is - ra -
6. O Fa - ther, Son and Spir - it

1. Lord, In God my Sa - vior
2. blest, For he has done great
3. fear From age to age and
4. throne And rai - ses those of
5. el, Re - mem - b'ring his e -
6. blest, In three - fold name are

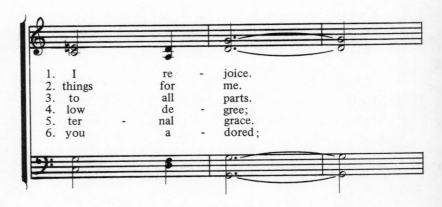

1. I re - joice.
2. things for me.
3. to all parts.
4. low de - gree;
5. ter - nal grace.
6. you a - dored;

1. My low - li - ness he did re -
2. Of all great names his is the
3. His arm of strength to all is
4. He feeds the hun - gry as his
5. As from of old he did for -
6. To you be ev - 'ry prayer ad -

1. gard, Ex - alt - ing me by
2. best. For it is ho - ly;
3. near; He scat - ters those who
4. own, The rich de - part in
5. tell To A - bra - ham and
6. drest, From age to age the

1. his own choice.
2. strong is he!
3. have proud hearts.
4. pov - er - ty.
5. to his race.
6. on - ly Lord.

PETITIONS Litany

Let us complete our evening prayer to the Lord.

All:

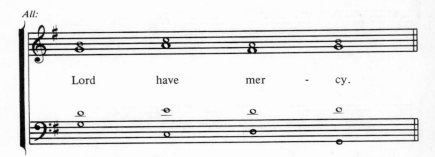

Lord have mer - cy.

For peace from on high and for our salvation, let us pray to the Lord.

For the welfare of all churches and for the unity of the human family, let us pray to the Lord.

For *(name)*, our bishop, and *(name)*, our pastor, and for all ministers of the Gospel, let us pray to the Lord.

For our nation, its government, and for all who serve and protect us, let us pray to the Lord.

For this city (town, university, monastery...), for every city and community, and for all those living in them, let us pray to the Lord.

For the good earth which God has given us and for the wisdom and will to conserve it, let us pray to the Lord.

For the safety of travelers, the recovery of the sick, the care of the destitute and the release of prisoners, let us pray to the Lord.

For an angel of peace to guide and protect us, let us pray to the Lord.

For a peaceful evening and a night free from sin, let us pray to the Lord.

For a Christian end to our lives and for all who have fallen asleep in Christ, let us pray to the Lord.

In the communion of the Holy Spirit (and of all the saints), let us commend ourselves and one another to the living God through Christ our Lord.

All:

To you, O Lord.

Free Prayer

In silent or spontaneous prayer all bring before God the concerns of the day.

154

Concluding Prayer

The leader brings the petitions to a close with an appropriate prayer:

Sunday
Lord Jesus Christ,
by your cross and resurrection,
you struck down death
and brought life to those in the grave.
May your blessed passion be the joy of the whole world
and the glory of your rising always be our song,
O Savior of the world,
living and reigning with the Father and Spirit,
now and for ever.

All:
Amen.

Friday
Heavenly Father,
from the pierced side of Christ came blood and water,
indelible signs of love made visible.
May the fountains of living water
which flow from his heart of love
quench the thirst of those
who seek you with all their strength.
You are one God for ever and ever.

All:
Amen.

Weekdays
Be our light in the darkness, O Lord,
and in your great mercy
defend us from the perils and dangers
of the night that lies before us;
for the love of your only Son,
our Savior Jesus Christ.

All:
Amen.

THE LORD'S PRAYER

Leader:

Gathering our praise and prayers into one, let us offer the prayer Christ himself taught us:

All may exend their hands as they pray.

Our Fa - ther in heav - en, hal - lowed be your name,

your king - dom come, your will be done,

on earth as in ___ heav - en. Give us to - day

our dai - ly bread. For - give us our sins

as we for - give those who sin ___ a - gainst ___ us.

Save us from the time of trial and de - liv - er

us from e - vil. For the king - dom the pow'r

and the glo - ry are yours, now and for ev - er.

Assistant:
Let us bow our heads to the Lord.

Leader:
May God, the Father almighty, bless us and keep us.

All:
Amen.

Leader:
May Jesus Christ, his only Son, our Lord, graciously smile upon us.

All:
Amen.

Leader:
May the Holy Spirit, the Lord and giver of life, grant us peace.

All:
Amen.

Sign of Peace

All may conclude the celebration by exchanging a sign of peace.

Evening Prayer

MUSICAL SETTING: HOWARD HUGHES, SM

The church or room is dimly lit as the service begins.

LIGHT Light Proclamation

All stand *The assistant stands before the candle and sings:*

Light and peace in Je - sus Christ our Lord.

All respond:

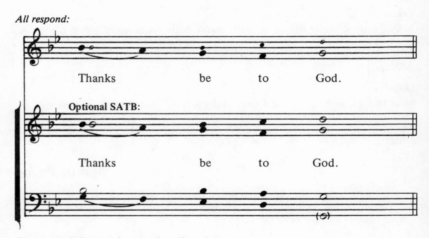

Thanks be to God.

Optional SATB:

Thanks be to God.

The electric lights may be turned up if needed.

Evening Hymn

O Radiant Light
Trans., W.G.S.

1. O   ra - diant Light, O   Sun di - vine,
2. O   Son of God, the Source of life,
3. Lord Je - sus Christ, as day - light fades,

1. Of God the Fa - ther's death - less face,
2. Praise is your due by night and day.
3. As shine the lights of e - ven - tide,

1. O   Im - age of the light sub - lime
2. Our hap - py lips must raise the strain
3. We praise the Fa - ther with the Son,

1. That fills the heav - 'nly dwell - ing place:
2. Of your es - teemed and splen - did name.
3. The Spir - it blest, and with them one.

159

Evening Thanksgiving

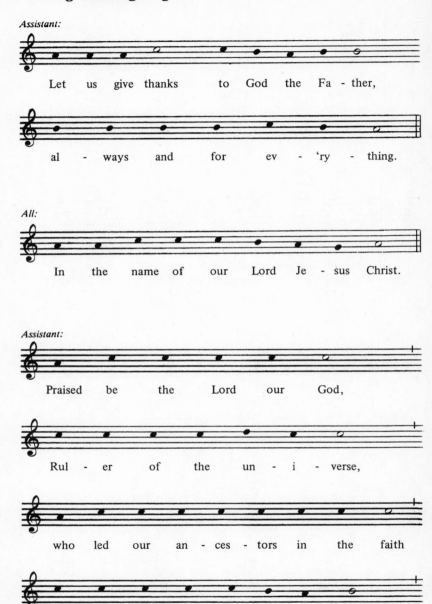

Assistant:

Let us give thanks to God the Fa - ther,

al - ways and for ev - 'ry - thing.

All:

In the name of our Lord Je - sus Christ.

Assistant:

Praised be the Lord our God,

Rul - er of the un - i - verse,

who led our an - ces - tors in the faith

by a pil - lar of cloud by day

and a pil - lar of fire by night,

and pre - pared a lamp for his A - noint - ed.

Light up our dark - ness, O God,

by the light of your Christ;

may his word be a lamp to our feet

and a light to our path,

for you are full of lov - ing kind - ness

for your whole cre - a - tion

and we, your crea - tures, glo - ri - fy you,

Fa - ther, Son and Ho - ly Spir - it,

All:

now and al - ways and for ev - er and ev - er. A - men.

INCENSE Psalm 140/141: Evening Prayer for Forgiveness and Protection

The psalms in this service are sung in a responsorial manner, i.e., the cantor sings the antiphon and all repeat it; the cantor sings the verses of the psalm and all repeat the antiphon as indicated. Some form of incensation may accompany the singing of this psalm.

Assistant:

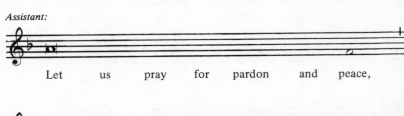

Let us pray for pardon and peace,

and for pro-tection throughout the com-ing night.

Antiphon

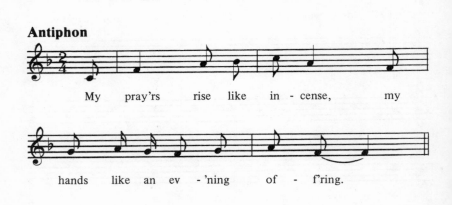

My pray'rs rise like in-cense, my

hands like an ev-'ning of-f'ring.

Verses

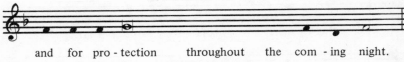

1. I call to you, O Lord; help me now!
2. Set a guard over my mouth, O Lord,
3. The good may chas-tise me.
4. Lord God, I look to you for help
5. Glory to the Father, and to the Son,

162

1. Listen to me, O Lord, I am in - vok - ing you.
2. a sentry at the door of my lips.
3. in their kind - ness re - buke me,
4. in you I take refuge; spare my life.
5. and to the Ho - ly Spir - it:

1. Let my prayer rise like incense be - fore you,
2. Save me from all wicked deeds and de - sires.
3. but the wicked shall never anoint my head with oil;
4. Keep me from the traps they have set for me,
5. as it was in the be - gin - ning,

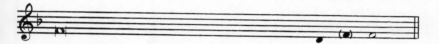

1. my uplifted hands like an evening ob - la - tion.
2. I will not feast with sin - ners.
3. my prayer rises ever a - gainst them.
4. save me from the snares of those who do e - vil.
5. is now, and will be for ever. A - men.

Psalm Prayer

The leader invites all to pray in silence for a moment:
Let us pray.

Then the leader offers one of the following prayers in the name of the community:

Sunday
Father of glory,
you raised our Lord Jesus Christ from the dead
and made him sit at your right hand in heaven.
Rescue us from our sins,
bring us to new life in him
and give us a place in heaven,
with the same Christ Jesus our Lord.

All:
Amen.

Friday
Almighty and everlasting God,
may our prayers rise like incense before you,
our hands like an evening sacrifice.
As we contemplate your presence in word and sacrament
and in the lives of those around us,
stir up in us the flame of that love
which Jesus kindled on earth by his passion
and which burns in our hearts by the Holy Spirit.
You are one God for ever and ever.

All:
Amen.

Weekdays
Look down, O Lord, from your heavenly throne,
and illumine the darkness of this coming night
with your celestial brightness;
from the children of light
banish the deeds of darkness,
through Jesus Christ our Lord.

All:
Amen.

Advent
To you, Lord God, our eyes are turned
as we stand in eager expectation
of that day when peace shall flow from Zion
and the deserts shall bloom with your justice.
As our prayers ascend to you like the fragrance of incense
may your glory come down upon us
in the kingdom of your Son
who will live and reign with you and the Holy Spirit,
for ever and ever.

All:
Amen.

Christmas

Lord of glory and Creator of all,
you anointed Jesus with your favor.
He has dwelt among us and become our offering.
Accept the gift of incense,
our prayer which rises before you.
Shed Christ's light upon the darkness of our hearts
and free us from all that is evil.
We ask this in the name of Jesus the Christ
who with the Holy Spirit and you
is worthy of all glory
now and for ever.

All:
Amen.

Lent

Lord God, our Father,
in this season of repentance
we beg you to receive our sacrifice of praise.
Throughout these forty days
may our voices cry to you in unceasing prayer,
our bodies abstain from the feasts of the wicked
and our hearts be turned to the needs of your people.
We ask this through Christ our Lord.

All:
Amen.

Easter

O God, our Father and Liberator,
Jesus Christ, your Son and our brother,
turned his eyes to you even in death.
You spared his soul
and anointed his head with glory.
May our prayers rise before you like incense
and our evening be the favored moment
of your peace and spirit,
in Jesus our risen Lord.

All:
Amen.

PSALMODY Psalm 120/121: We Are a Pilgrim People

All are seated *Psalm 120/121, some other evening psalm or a New Testament Canticle may be sung at this point.*

Antiphon

Our help comes from the Lord, the

mak - er of heav - en and earth.

Verses

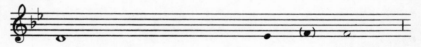

1. I lift up my eyes to the moun - tains:
2. May he never allow you to stum - ble!
3. The Lord is your guard and your shade;
4. The Lord will guard you from e - vil;
5. Glory to the Father, and to the Son,

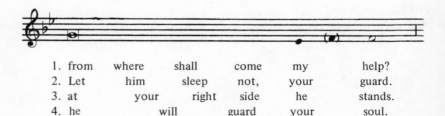

1. from where shall come my help?
2. Let him sleep not, your guard.
3. at your right side he stands.
4. he will guard your soul.
5. and to the Ho - ly Spir - it:

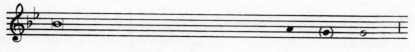

1. My help shall come from the Lord
2. No, he sleeps not nor slum - bers,
3. By day the sun shall not smite you
4. The Lord will ᐟ guard your going and com - ing
5. as it was in the be - gin - ning,

1. who made heaven and earth.
2. Isra - el's guard.
3. nor the moon in the night.
4. both now and for ever.
5. is now, and will be for ever. A - men.

Psalm Prayer

The leader invites everyone to pray in silence for a moment:
Let us pray.

Then the leader offers the following psalm prayer in the name of the community:
Lord Jesus Christ,
you have prepared a place for us
in your Father's eternal home.
Watch over our welfare on this perilous journey,
guard us from life's dangers,
and keep our lives free from evil until the end.
Yours is the power and the glory for ever and ever.

All:
Amen.

All stand Psalm 116/117: A Doxology

The evening psalmody may be concluded with Psalm 116/117 or some other doxology.

Antiphon

168

1. O praise the Lord, all you na - tions,
ac - claim him all you peo - ples!
Strong is his love for us;
he is faith - ful for ev - er.
Antiphon

2. Give glo - ry to the Fa - ther al - might-y,
to his Son, Je - sus Christ, the Lord,
To the Spir - it who dwells in our hearts,
both now and for ev - er. A - men.
Antiphon

There is no psalm prayer after this psalm.

THE WORD
OF GOD

All are seated *A reader proclaims the word of God.*

Brothers and sisters,
I beg of you through the mercy of God
to offer your bodies as a living sacrifice
holy and acceptable to God, your spiritual worship.
Do not conform yourselves to this age
but be transformed by the renewal of your mind,
so that you may judge what is God's will,
what is good, pleasing and perfect. *(Romans 12:1-2)*

At the end of the reading, the reader raises the Bible and says:
This is the word of the Lord.

All respond:
Thanks be to God.

After the reading, all pray in silence, opening their minds and hearts to the Spirit.

Other brief readings:

Romans 5:6-11
1 Corinthians 9:24-27
Galatians 6:7-10
Ephesians 6:10-18
Philippians 4:4-9
Colossians 3:12-17
Titus 2:11-14
1 Timothy 6:12-16
Hebrews 12:1-2
I Peter 5:6-11
1 John 4:7-12
Revelations 22:1-5

Canticle of Mary (Lk. 1:46-55)

During this song, the altar and the community may be honored with incense. All make a sign **All stand**
of the cross as the canticle begins:

Trans., J. T. Mueller, 1940, alt.

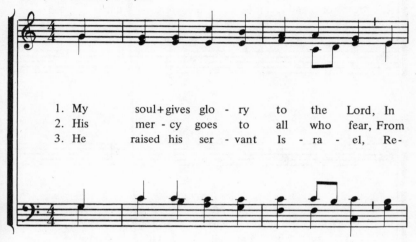

1. My soul+gives glo - ry to the Lord, In
2. His mer - cy goes to all who fear, From
3. He raised his ser - vant Is - ra - el, Re-

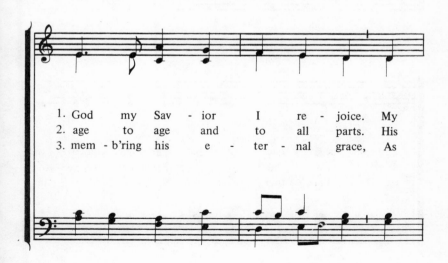

1. God my Sav - ior I re - joice. My
2. age to age and to all parts. His
3. mem - b'ring his e - ter - nal grace, As

171

1. low - li - ness he did re - gard, Ex -
3. arm of strength to all is near; He
5. from of old he did fore - tell To

1. alt - ing me by his own choice.
3. scat - ters those who have proud hearts.
5. A - bra - ham and all his race.

2. From this day all shall call me blest, For
4. He casts the might - y from their throne And
6. O Fa - ther, Son and Spir - it blest, In

172

2. he has done great things for me. Of
4. rais - es those of low de - gree; He
6. three - fold Name you are a - dored; To

2. all great names his is the best, For
4. feeds the hun - gry as his own; The
6. you be ev - 'ry pray'r ad - drest, From

2. it is ho - ly; strong is he.
4. rich de - part in pov - er - ty.
6. age to age the on - ly Lord. *(Repeat stanza one)*

N.B. These two melodies may be antiphonated between any combination of congregation, cantor, and choir.

PETITIONS Litany

Assistant:

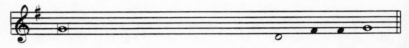

Let us complete our evening prayer to the Lord.

All:

Lord have mer - cy.

For peace from on high and for our salvation, let us pray to the Lord.
For the welfare of all churches and for the unity of the human family,
    let us pray to the Lord.
For *(name),* our bishop, and *(name),* our pastor, and for all ministers
    of the Gospel, let us pray to the Lord.
For our nation, its government, and for all who serve and protect us,
    let us pray to the Lord.
For this city (town, university, monastery...), for every city and
    community, and for all those living in them, let us pray to the Lord.
For the good earth which God has given us and for the wisdom and
    will to conserve it, let us pray to the Lord.
For the safety of travelers, the recovery of ths sick, the care of the
    destitute and the release of prisoners, let us pray to the Lord.
For an angel of peace to guide and protect us, let us pray to the Lord.
For a peaceful evening and a night free from sin, let us pray
    to the Lord.
For a Christian end to our lives and for all who have fallen asleep in
    Christ, let us pray to the Lord.
In the communion of the Holy Spirit (and of all the saints), let us
    commend ourselves and one another to the living God through
    Christ our Lord.

All:
To you, O Lord.

Free Prayer

In silent or spontaneous prayer all bring before God the concerns of the day.

Concluding Prayer

The leader brings the petitions to a close with an appropriate prayer:

Sunday
Lord Jesus Christ,
by your cross and resurrection,
you struck down death
and brought life to those in the grave.
May your blessed passion be the joy of the whole world
and the glory of your rising always be our song,
O Savior of the world,
living and reigning with the Father and Spirit,
now and for ever.

All:
Amen.

Friday
Heavenly Father,
from the pierced side of Christ came blood and water,
indelible signs of love made visible.
May the fountains of living water
which flow from his heart of love
quench the thirst of those
who seek you with all their strength.
You are one God for ever and ever.

All:
Amen.

Weekdays
Be our light in the darkness, O Lord,
and in your great mercy
defend us from the perils and dangers
of the night that lies before us;
for the love of your only Son,
our Savior Jesus Christ.

All:
Amen.

THE LORD'S PRAYER

Leader:

Gathering our praise and prayers into one, let us offer the prayer Christ himself taught us:

All may extend their hands as they pray:

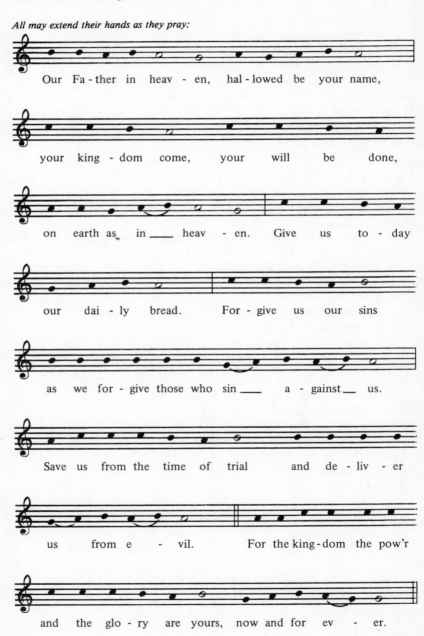

Our Fa - ther in heav - en, hal - lowed be your name,

your king - dom come, your will be done,

on earth as in ___ heav - en. Give us to - day

our dai - ly bread. For - give us our sins

as we for - give those who sin ___ a - gainst ___ us.

Save us from the time of trial and de - liv - er

us from e - vil. For the king - dom the pow'r

and the glo - ry are yours, now and for ev - er.

Assistant:
Let us bow our heads to the Lord.

Leader: *All:*

1. _____
2. _____   A - men! A - men!
3. _____

Leader:
May God, the Father almighty, bless us and keep us.

All:
Amen.

Leader:
May Jesus Christ, his only Son, our Lord, graciously smile upon us.

All:
Amen.

Leader:
May the Holy Spirit, the Lord and giver of life, grant us peace.

All:
Amen.

Sign of Peace

All may conclude the celebration by exchanging a sign of peace.

Evening Prayer

MUSICAL SETTING: MICHAEL JONCAS

The church or room is dimly lit as the service begins.

LIGHT Light Proclamation

All stand *The assistant stands before the candle and sings:*

Light and peace in Je - sus Christ our Lord.

All respond:

Thanks be to God.

The electric lights may be turned up if needed.

Evening Hymn

O Radiant Light
Trans., W.G.S.

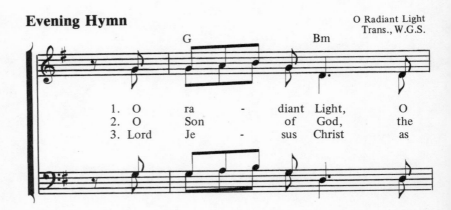

1. O ra - diant Light, O
2. O Son of God, the
3. Lord Je - sus Christ as

178

1. Sun di - vine, Of God the Fa - ther's
2. Source of life, Praise is your due by
3. day - light fades, as shine the lights of

1. death - less face, O Im - age of the
2. night and day. Our hap - py lips must
3. ev - en - tide, We praise the Fa - ther

1. Light sub - lime that fills the heav'n - ly
2. raise the strain of your es - teem'd and
3. with the Son, the Spir - it blest and

1. dwell - ing place.
2. splen - did name.
3. with them one.

179

Evening Thanksgiving

Assistant:

Let us give thanks to God our Fa - ther,

al - ways and for ev - 'ry - thing:

All:

In the name of Our Lord Je - sus Christ.

Assistant:

Praised be the Lord our God, Rul - er of the un - i - verse,

who led our ancestors in the faith

180

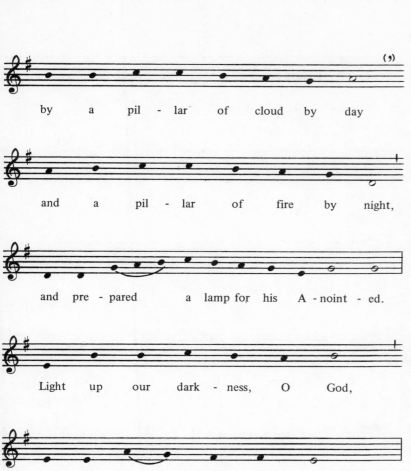

by a pil - lar of cloud by day

and a pil - lar of fire by night,

and pre - pared a lamp for his A - noint - ed.

Light up our dark - ness, O God,

by the light of your Christ;

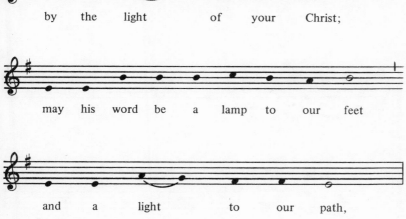

may his word be a lamp to our feet

and a light to our path,

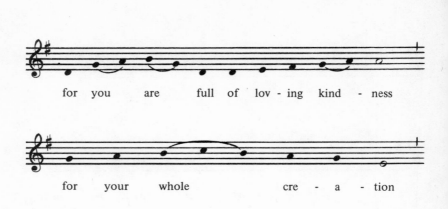

for you are full of lov - ing kind - ness

for your whole cre - a - tion

and we, your crea - tures, glo - ri - fy you,

Fa - ther, Son and Ho - ly Spir - it,

now and for - ev - er.

All:

A - men. A - men.

182

Psalm 140/141: Evening Prayer for Forgiveness and   INCENSE
Protection

The psalms in this service are sung in a responsorial manner, i.e., the cantor sings the antiphon and all repeat it; then the cantor sings the verses of the psalm and all repeat the antiphon as indicated. Some form of incensation may accompany the singing of this psalm.

Assistant:

Let us pray for par - don and peace,

and for pro - tect - tion through - out the com - ing night.

Antiphon

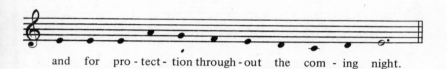

Am   Dm   Am

My prayers rise like in - cense;   my

Soprano
Alto
Ah.
Tenor
Bass

F   C   E7

hands like the eve - ning of - fer - ing.

S/A
Ah
T/B

183

Verses

1. I call to you, O Lord; help me now!

Listen to me, O Lord, I am in - vok - ing you.

Let my prayer rise like in - cense be - fore you,

my up - lift - ed hands like an eve - ning ob - la - tion. *Antiphon*

2. Set a guard over my mouth, O Lord,

a sentry at the door of my lips.

Save me from all wick - ed deeds and de - sires.

I will not feast with sin - ners. *Antiphon*

3. The good may chas - tise me,

in their kind - ness re - buke me,

184

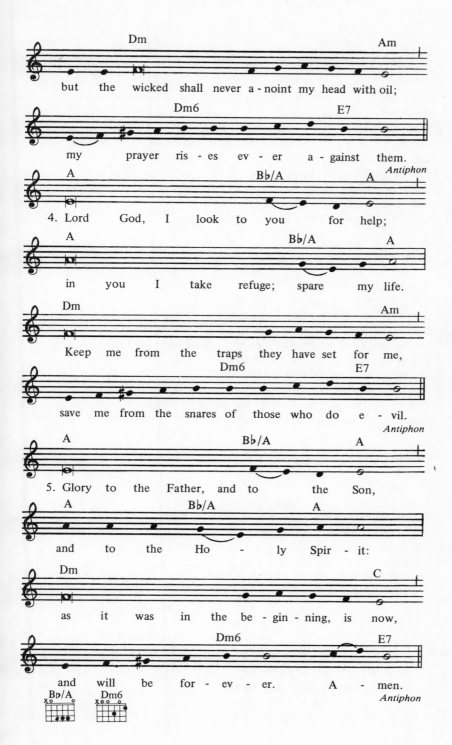

Dm   Am

but   the   wicked   shall   never a - noint my head with oil;

Dm6   E7

my   prayer ris - es   ev - er   a - gainst   them.

A   Bb/A   A   *Antiphon*

4. Lord   God,   I   look   to   you   for   help;

A   Bb/A   A

in   you   I   take   refuge;   spare   my   life.

Dm   Am

Keep   me   from   the   traps   they have set   for   me,

Dm6   E7

save   me from the   snares   of   those who do   e - vil.

                                      Antiphon

A   Bb/A   A

5. Glory   to   the   Father, and to   the   Son,

A   Bb/A   A

and   to   the   Ho -   ly   Spir - it:

Dm   C

as   it   was   in   the   be - gin - ning, is   now,

Dm6   E7

and   will   be   for - ev - er.   A - men.

                                     Antiphon

Bb/A   Dm6

185

Psalm Prayer

The leader invites all to pray in silence for a moment:
Let us pray.

Then the leader offers one of the following prayers in the name of the community:
Sunday
Father of glory,
you raised our Lord Jesus Christ from the dead
and made him sit at your right hand in heaven.
Rescue us from our sins,
bring us to new life in him
and give us a place in heaven,
with the same Christ Jesus our Lord.

All:
Amen.

Friday
Almighty and everlasting God,
may our prayers rise like incense before you,
our hands like an evening sacrifice.
As we contemplate your presence in word and sacrament
and in the lives of those around us,
stir up in us the flame of that love
which Jesus kindled on earth by his passion
and which burns in our hearts by the Holy Spirit.
You are one God for ever and ever.

All:
Amen.

Weekdays
Look down, O Lord, from your heavenly throne,
and illumine the darkness of this coming night
with your celestial brightness;
from the children of light
banish the deeds of darkness,
through Jesus Christ our Lord.

All:
Amen.

Advent
To you, Lord God, our eyes are turned
as we stand in eager expectation
of that day when peace shall flow from Zion
and the deserts shall bloom with your justice.
As our prayers ascend to you like the fragrance of incense

may your glory come down upon us
in the kingdom of your Son
who will live and reign with you and the Holy Spirit
for ever and ever.

All:
Amen.

Christmas

Lord of glory and Creator of all,
you anointed Jesus with your favor.
He has dwelt among us and become our offering.
Accept the gift of incense,
our prayer which rises before you.
Shed Christ's light upon the darkness of our hearts
and free us from all that is evil.
We ask this in the name of Jesus the Christ
who with the Holy Spirit and you
is worthy of all glory now and for ever.

All:
Amen.

Lent

Lord God, our Father,
in this season of repentance
we beg you to receive our sacrifice of praise.
Throughout these forty days
may our voices cry to you in unceasing prayer,
our bodies abstain from the feasts of the wicked
and our hearts be turned to the needs of your people.
We ask this through Christ our Lord.

All:
Amen.

Easter

O God, our Father and Liberator,
Jesus Christ, your Son and our brother,
turned his eyes to you even in death.
You spared his soul
and anointed his head with glory.
May our prayers rise before you like incense
and our evening be the favored moment
of your peace and spirit,
in Jesus our risen Lord.

All:
Amen.

187

PSALMODY Psalm 120/121: We Are a Pilgrim People

All are seated *Psalm 120/121, some other evening psalm or a New Testament Canticle may be sung at this point.*

Antiphon

Our help comes from the Lord, the mak-er of heav-en and earth.

Verses

1. I lift up my eyes to the moun-tains: from where shall come my help? My help shall come from the Lord who made heav-en and earth.

Antiphon

2. May he nev-er al-low you to stum-ble! Let him sleep not, your guard.

No, he sleeps not, nor slum - bers,

He, Is - ra - el's guard.

Antiphon

3. The Lord is your guard and your shade;

at your right side he stands.

By day the sun shall not smite you nor the

moon in the night.

Antiphon

4. The Lord will guard you from e - vil;

he will guard your soul.

AM7   Bm/A   F#m   F#m7   B   Bm7

189

The Lord will guard your go-ing and com-ing
both now and for-ev-er.

Antiphon

5. Glo-ry to the Fa-ther, and to the
Son, and to the Ho-ly Spir-it:
as it was in the be-gin-ning, is now,
and will be for-ev-er. A-men.

Antiphon

Psalm Prayer

The leader invites everyone to pray in silence for a moment:
Let us pray.

Then the leader offers the following psalm prayer in the name of the community:
Lord Jesus Christ,
you have prepared a place for us
in your Father's eternal home.
Watch over our welfare on this perilous journey,
guard us from life's dangers,
and keep our lives free from evil until the end.
Yours is the power and the glory for ever and ever.

All:
Amen.

190

Psalm 116/117: A Doxology All stand

The evening psalmody may be concluded with Psalm 116/117 or some other doxology.

Assistant:

Let us lift up our voic - es,

and glo - ri - fy the liv - ing God.

Antiphon

Ho - ly is God!

Ho - ly is

Ho - ly and strong! Ho-ly is God!

God! Ho - ly! Ho - ly! Ho-ly is God!

Ho - ly and strong! Ho - ly and liv - ing for - ev - er!

Ho - ly and strong! Ho - ly and liv - ing for - ev - er!

Verses

1. O praise the Lord, all you na - tions, ac -
claim him all you peo - ples! Strong is his
love for us, he is faith - ful for - ev - er - more!

Antiphon

2. Give glo - ry to the Fa - ther Al - might - y, to his
Son Je - sus Christ the Lord. To the Spir - it who
dwells in our hearts, both now and for - ev - er. A - men!

Antiphon

There is no psalm prayer after this psalm.

192

A reader proclaims the word of God.

Brothers and sisters,
I beg you through the mercy of God
to offer your bodies as a living sacrifice
holy and acceptable to God, your spiritual worship.
Do not conform yourselves to this age
but be transformed by the renewal of your mind,
so that you may judge what is God's will,
what is good, pleasing and perfect. *(Romans 12:1-2)*

At the end of the reading, the reader raises the Bible and says:
This is the word of the Lord.

All respond:
Thanks be to God.

After the reading, all pray in silence, opening their minds and hearts to the Spirit.

Other brief readings:

Romans 5:6-11

1 Corinthians 9:24-27

Galatians 6:7-10

Ephesians 6:10-18

Philippians 4:4-9

Colossians 3:12-17

Titus 2:11-14

1 Timothy 6:12-16

Hebrews 12:1-2

1 Peter 5:6-11

1 John 4:7-12

Revelations 22:1-5

CANTICLE
OF PRAISE Canticle of Mary (Lk. 1:46-55)

All stand *During this song, the altar and the community may be honored with incense. All make a sign of the cross as the canticle begins.*

Trans., J. T. Mueller, 1940, alt.

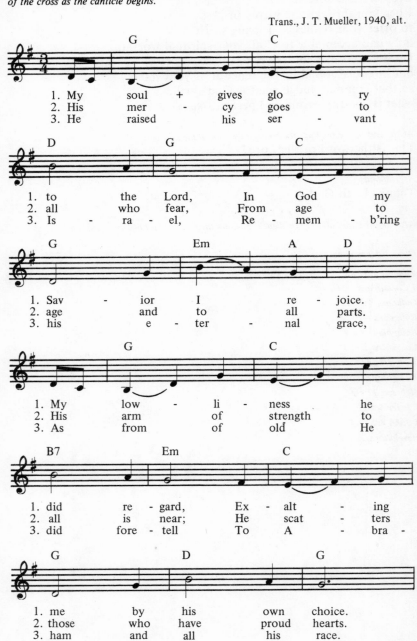

G   C

1. My   soul   +   gives   glo   -   ry
2. His   mer   -   cy   goes   to
3. He   raised   his   ser   -   vant

D   G   C

1. to   the   Lord,   In   God   my
2. all   who   fear,   From   age   to
3. Is   -   ra   -   el,   Re   -   mem   -   b'ring

G   Em   A   D

1. Sav   -   ior   I   re   -   joice.
2. age   and   to   all   parts.
3. his   e   -   ter   -   nal   grace,

G   C

1. My   low   -   li   -   ness   he
2. His   arm   of   strength   to
3. As   from   of   old   He

B7   Em   C

1. did   re   -   gard,   Ex   -   alt   -   ing
2. all   is   near;   He   scat   -   ters
3. did   fore   -   tell   To   A   -   bra   -

G   D   G

1. me   by   his   own   choice.
2. those   who   have   proud   hearts.
3. ham   and   all   his   race.

194

1. From this day all shall
2. He casts the might - y
3. O Fa - ther, Son and

1. call me blest, For he has
2. from their throne And rais - es
3. Spir - it blest, In three - fold

1. done great things for me,
2. those of low de - gree;
3. Name are you a - dored,

1. Of all great names his
2. He feeds the hun - gry
3. To you be ev - 'ry

1. is the best, For it is
2. as his own, The rich de -
3. prayer ad - drest, From age to

1. ho - ly; strong is he.
2. part in po - ver - ty.
3. age the on - ly Lord.

195

PETITIONS Litany

Assistant:

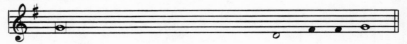

Let us complete our evening prayer to the Lord.

All:

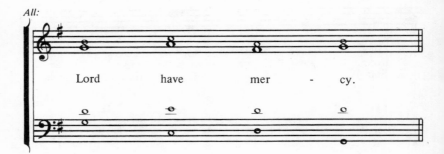

Lord have mer - cy.

For peace from on high and for our salvation, let us pray to the Lord.

For the welfare of all churches and for the unity of the human family, let us pray to the Lord.

For *(name)*, our bishop, and *(name)*, our pastor, and for all ministers of the Gospel, let us pray to the Lord.

For our nation, its government, and for all who serve and protect us, let us pray to the Lord.

For this city (town, university, monastery . . .), for every city and community, and for all those living in them, let us pray to the Lord.

For the good earth which God has given us and for the wisdom and will to conserve it, let us pray to the Lord.

For the safety of travelers, the recovery of the sick, the care of the destitute and the release of prisoners, let us pray to the Lord.

For an angel of peace to guide and protect us, let us pray to the Lord.

For a peaceful evening and a night free from sin, let us pray to the Lord.

For a Christian end to our lives and for all who have fallen asleep in Christ, let us pray to the Lord.

In the communion of the Holy Spirit (and of all the saints), let us commend ourselves and one another to the living God through Christ our Lord.

All respond:
To you, O Lord.

Free Prayer

In silent or spontaneous prayer all bring before God the concerns of the day.

Concluding Prayer

The leader brings the petitions to a close with an appropriate prayer:

Sunday
Lord Jesus Christ,
by your cross and resurrection,
you struck down death
and brought life to those in the grave.
May your blessed passion be the joy of the whole world
and the glory of your rising always be our song,
O Savior of the world,
living and reigning with the Father and Spirit,
now and for ever.

All:
Amen.

Friday
Heavenly Father,
from the pierced side of Christ came blood and water,
indelible signs of love made visible.
May the fountains of living water
which flow from his heart of love
quench the thirst of those
who seek you with all their strength.
You are one God for ever and ever.

All:
Amen.

Weekdays
Be our light in the darkness, O Lord,
and in your great mercy
defend us from the perils and dangers
of the night that lies before us;
for the love of your only Son,
our Savior Jesus Christ.

All:
Amen.

THE LORD'S PRAYER

Leader:

Gathering our praise and prayers into one, let us offer the prayer Christ himself taught us:

All may extend their hands as they pray:

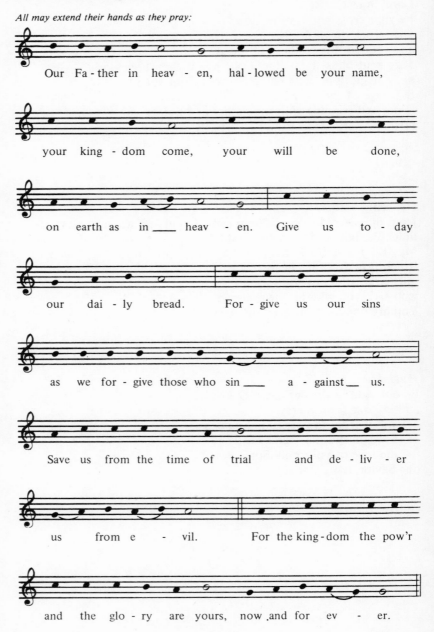

Our Fa - ther in heav - en, hal - lowed be your name, your king - dom come, your will be done, on earth as in ___ heav - en. Give us to - day our dai - ly bread. For - give us our sins as we for - give those who sin ___ a - gainst ___ us. Save us from the time of trial and de - liv - er us from e - vil. For the king - dom the pow'r and the glo - ry are yours, now and for ev - er.

198

Assistant:
Let us bow our heads to the Lord.

Leader: *All:*

1.
2.
3.   A - men! A - men!

Leader:
May God, the Father almighty, bless us and keep us.

All:
Amen.

Leader:
May Jesus Christ, his only Son, our Lord, graciously smile upon us.

All:
Amen.

Leader:
May the Holy Spirit, the Lord and giver of life, grant us peace.

All:
Amen.

Sign of Peace

All may conclude the celebration by exchanging a sign of peace.

Evening Prayer

BRIEF FORM

(at meal time)

SERVICE NOTES

Evening Prayer is a service of praise, which gives thanks to the Lord for blessings received throughout the day, and asks for protection throughout the later evening.

Prayer at meal times is part of our Christian heritage and our debt to our Jewish ancestors. For the Christian to pray at meal times is quite natural. The entire setting of the Last Supper speaks of the connection between prayer and the sharing of food and drink. Understanding the sacramentality of the shared meal is heightened through this form or prayer. It aids the community to see the deeper significance of joining together to share food, drink and the sustaining Word of the Lord.

Light

The evening prayer and hymn blesses God for the gift of light, for the sun of the day and for the Son of God, Light itself.

Psalmody

Themes of trust, peace and thanksgiving characterize the evening psalms. If at all possible, psalms should be sung. Cf. remarks on psalmody given in the introduction to Morning Prayer.

The Word of God

The selections given speak of the meals shared among the followers of Jesus. It is possible to choose other brief readings for the service.

Response

The prayer prayed by the leader gives thanks to the Lord and introduces the symbolic sharing of the bread and/or cup, as a sign of fellowship in his name.

Sharing of the Meal

The sharing of the meal follows.

Petitions

After the meal is finished, intercessory prayer is offered. Various forms for this prayer may be used.

The Lord's Prayer

The Lord's Prayer, a prayer of praise, blessing and petition, concludes the intercessory prayer.

Blessing

A brief blessing, prayed by the leader, ends the service. Any short blessing may be used.

Sign of Peace

If appropriate, a sign of peace may be shared.

 # Evening Prayer

BRIEF FORM *(at meal time)*

LIGHT

All stand *The dining room is dimly lit. All take their places at table. We praise Christ, the true light of the world. The leader lights the candle which is in a prominent place on or near the table. As the candle is lit, the leader proclaims:*

Light and peace in Jesus Christ our Lord.

All respond:
Thanks be to God.

The leader continues:
Eternal God,
you led your ancient people into freedom
with a pillar of cloud by day
and a pillar of fire by night.
Grant that we who walk in the light of your presence
may rejoice in the liberty of the children of God;
through Jesus Christ our Lord.

All respond:
Amen.

Evening Hymn

As the lights are lit, the evening hymn is sung.

Plainsong
Jesu, dulcis memoria
Trans., W.G.S.

1. O   ra - diant   Light,   O   Sun   di - vine
2. O   Son   of   God,   the   source   of   life,
3. Lord   Je - sus   Christ,   as   day - light   fades,

1. Of   God   the   Fa - ther's   death - less   face,
2. Praise   is   your   due   by   night   and   day.
3. As   shine   the   lights   of   e - ven - tide,

1. O   im - age   of   the   light   sub - lime
2. Our   hap - py   lips   must   raise   the   strain
3. We   praise   the   Fa - ther   with   the   Son,

1. That   fills   the   heav'n - ly   dwell - ing   place:
2. Of   your   es - teem'd   and   splen - did   name.
3. The   Spir - it   blest,   and   with   them   one.

203

PSALMODY

All are seated *One of the following evening psalms is prayed.*

Psalm 140/141: Evening Prayer for Forgiveness and Protection

Antiphon

J.A.M.

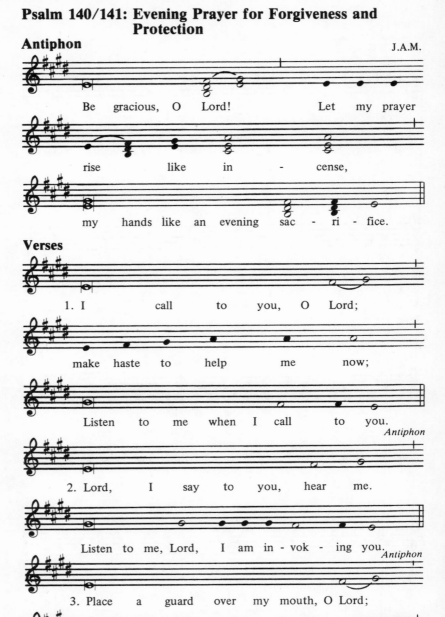

Be gracious, O Lord! Let my prayer

rise like in - cense,

my hands like an evening sac - ri - fice.

Verses

1. I call to you, O Lord;

make haste to help me now;

Listen to me when I call to you.
Antiphon

2. Lord, I say to you, hear me.

Listen to me, Lord, I am in - vok - ing you. *Antiphon*

3. Place a guard over my mouth, O Lord;

204

keep my heart from in - clin - ing to e - vil;

save me from all wicked deeds and de-sires.
Antiphon

4. May the righteous reprove me in kind-ness,

but I will not let the wick-ed a-noint my head;

I will always resist their e-vil deeds.
Antiphon

5. Lord God, my eyes are turned to you,

de-fend and pro-tect me, in you I take ref-uge.
Antiphon

6. Glory to the Father and to the Son,

and to the Spir-it, as it was in the beginning,

is now, and will be for ev-er.
Antiphon

Psalm Prayer

The leader invites everyone to pray in silence for a moment:

Let us pray.

Then the leader offers the following psalm prayer in the name of the community:

In your mercy
hear our evening prayer, O God of compassion,
that freed from the darkness of sin,
we may always walk in your light,
through Jesus Christ our Lord.

All:

Amen.

Psalm 42/43 (adapted): To You I Life Up My Soul

Antiphon

John Kavanaugh, S.J.

To You I lift up my

soul, O Lord; in you, O my

God, I trust.

Verses

1. O send forth your light and send forth your
2. And we shall go to the al - tar of

truth, and let them be our
God, the God of our life and our

guide.
joy.

Let them lead us un -
And we shall

to your ho - ly moun-tain, Lord, to the
sing his praise on the harp, through

place where - on you dwell. *Antiphon*
all the days of our life. *Antiphon*

3. Praise the Fa - ther, the Son and the

Spir - it on high, both now and for -

ev - er. A - men. *Antiphon*

Psalm Prayer

The leader invites everyone to pray in silence for a moment:
Let us pray.

Then the leader offers the following psalm prayer in the name of the community:
Blessed are you, Lord, our God,
for you call us to be your people
and protect us as your chosen ones.
We offer our prayers to you this night
for your continued kindness;
through Jesus Christ our Lord.

All:
Amen.

Psalm 138/139 (adapted): You Are Near

Antiphon

Dan Schutte, S.J.

Yah - weh, I know you are near, stand - ing al - ways at my side. You guard me from the foe, and you lead me in ways ev - er - last - ing.

Verses

1. Lord, you have searched my heart, and you know when I sit and when I stand. Your hand is up - on me pro - tect - ing me from death,

Am7 *slowing*   Am7/G   D/F♯   *ritard.*

keep - ing me from harm.   *Antiphon*

G   C9   D/F♯

2. Where can I run from your love?   If I

Em   Am   Bm

climb to the heav - ens you are there;   if I

Bm   Em   Am   Bm

fly to the sun - rise or sail be - yond the sea,

Am7   *slowing*   Am7/E   D/F♯   *ritard.*

still I'd find you there.   *Antiphon*

G   C9   D/F♯

3. You know my heart and its ways,   you who

Em   Am   Bm

formed me be - fore I was born   in

Bm   Em   Am   Bm

se - cret of dark - ness be - fore I saw the sun

Am7 *slowing*   **Am7/G**   **D/F♯**   *ritard.*

in my moth - er's womb.   *Antiphon*

G   C9   D/F♯

4. Mar - vel - ous to me are your works; how pro -

Em   Am   Bm

found are your thoughts, my Lord, E - ven

Bm   Em   Am   Bm

if I could count them, they num - ber as the stars,

Am7 *slowing*   **Am7/G**   **D/F♯**

you would still be there.   *Antiphon*

Psalm Prayer

The leader invites everyone to pray in silence for a moment:
Let us pray.

Then the leader offers the following psalm prayer in the name of the community:
Lord God,
you are near to all who call upon you.
Guide and guard us this night
in the path to life everlasting;
through Jesus Christ our Lord.

All:
Amen.

210

A Scripture passage is proclaimed by the reader:
I received from the Lord what I handed on to you,
namely, that the Lord Jesus on the night in which he was betrayed
took bread, and after he had given thanks, broke it and said,
"This is my body, which is for you. Do this in remembrance of me."
In the same way, after the supper, he took the cup, saying,
"This cup is the new covenant in my blood.
Do this, whenever you drink it, in remembrance of me."
Every time, then, you eat this bread and drink this cup,
you proclaim the death of the Lord until he comes! *(I Cor. 11:23-26)*

At the end of the reading, the reader raises the Bible and says:
This is the word of the Lord.

All respond:
Thanks be to God.

All pray in silence, opening their minds and hearts to the Spirit.

Other brief readings:
Matthew 15:32-38
Matthew 22:1-10
Mark 8:1-10
Luke 14:16-24
Luke 24:13, 24-32
Luke 24:33-35
Luke 24:36b-43
John 21:4-8
John 21:9-14
John 21:15-17

RESPONSE *Then the leader says:*

Blessed are you, Lord our God,
for your word which gives us life.
Blessed are you, Lord of life,
for you give food to all who call upon you.
May our sharing of this meal reveal your loving kindness
and may your name be praised as we share this cup of wine.

[AND/OR]

Blessed are you, Lord our God,
for your word which gives us life.
Blessed are you, Lord of life,
for you give food to all who call upon you.
May our sharing of this meal reveal your loving kindness
and may your name be praised as we share this bread of life.

The cup of wine is shared by all and/or the bread is broken and given to all.

SHARING OF THE MEAL *All partake of the common meal as usual.*

PETITIONS *After the meal the leader prays:*

We give thanks to you, our God,
for good gifts which nourish us.
Because of your faithfulness,
we make known to you our needs.

Petitions may be voiced by all.

The leader concludes the petitions:

Grant our requests, as you see fit,
loving Father
for they are made in the name of Jesus,
who lives and reigns with you and the Spirit,
one God, for ever and ever.

All respond:
Amen.

THE LORD'S PRAYER

Leader:

With the Spirit in our hearts who cries "Abba, Father," let us pray:

All pray the Lord's Prayer.

BLESSING

Leader:

May the God of life continually show us his mercy revealed in the Lord Jesus.

All respond:

Amen.

Evening Supplement

Evening Hymn

D.C.I.

Trans., W.G.S.

1. O ra - diant Light, O Sun di-
2. O Son of God, the Source of
3. Lord Je - sus Christ, as day - light

1. vine, of God the Fa - ther's
2. life, praise is your due by
3. fades, as shine the lights of

1. death - less face, O
2. night and day. Our
3. e - ven tide, We

1. Im - age of the Light sub -
2. hap - py lips must raise the
3. praise the Fa - ther with the

1. lime that fills the heav'n - ly
2. strain of your es - teemed and
3. Son, the Spir - it blest, and

1. dwell - ing place:
2. splen - did name.
3. with them one.

Evening Hymn

Book of Common Prayer, 1979
Robert Edward Smith

O gra - cious Light, pure bright-ness of the

ev - er - liv - ing Fa - ther in heav - en,

O Je - sus Christ, ho - ly and bless - ed!

Now as we come to the set - ting of the

sun,   and our   eyes be - hold the   ves - per light,

we   sing your   prais - es   O

God: Fa - ther,   Son and Ho - ly   Spir - it.

You   are   wor - thy at   all times to   be

praised by hap - py voic - es,

O Son of God, O Giv - er of

Life, and to be glo -

- ri - fied through all the worlds.

218

Thanksgiving (Ordinary Time)

J.A.M.
Apostolic Constitutions

Assistant:

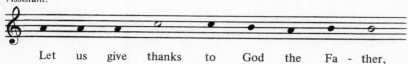

Let us give thanks to God the Fa - ther,

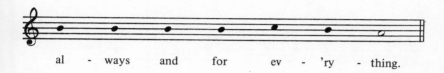

al - ways and for ev - 'ry - thing.

All:

In the name of our Lord Je - sus Christ.

Assistant:

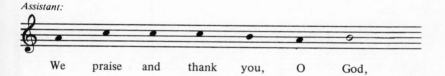

We praise and thank you, O God,

for you are with - out be - gin - ning and with - out end.

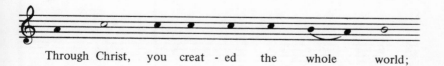

Through Christ, you creat - ed the whole world;

through Christ, you pre - serve it.

219

You are his God and Fa - ther,

the Giv - er of the Spir - it,

the Rul - er of all that is seen and un - seen.

You made the day for the works of light

and the night for the re - fresh - ment

of our minds and our bod - ies. O lov - ing Lord

and source of all that is good,

gra - cious-ly ac - cept our eve - ning sac - ri - fice of praise.

You have con - duct - ed us through the day

and brought us to night's be - gin - ning.

Keep us now in Christ, grant us a peace - ful

eve - ning and a night free from sin,

and bring us at last to e - ter - nal life.

Through Christ and in the Ho - ly Spir - it,

we of - fer you all glo - ry, hon - or and

All:

wor - ship, now and for ev - er.   A - men.

Thanksgiving (Ordinary Time)

J.A.M.

Assistant:

Let us give thanks to God the Fa - ther,

al - ways and for ev - 'ry - thing.

All:

In the name of our Lord Je - sus Christ.

Assistant:

Bless - ed are you, O Lord our God,

the Cre - a - tor and Rul - er of all that ex - ists.

You shaped the heav - ens and dai - ly bless us

with their ra - diant light, the sac - ra - ment of that

un - dy - ing light, which fills our hearts and minds.

As night ap-proach-es, we thank you for the pow-er to cre-ate the light which dis-pels the dark-ness a-round us. Be with us still, en-light-en our hearts with your glo-ry and lead us to the full-ness of your splen-dor. All hon-or and bless-ing be to you, through Je-sus Christ, the light of the world, and in the Ho-ly Spir-it, who en-a-bles us to sing your praise now and for ev-er.

All: A-men.

Thanksgiving (Ordinary Time)

J.A.M.
Jewish Berakah of the Evening

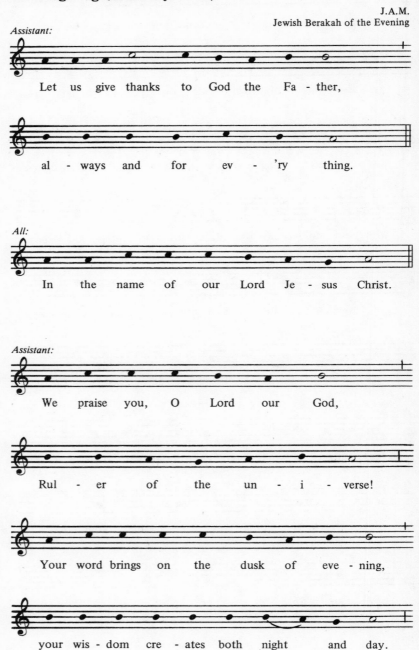

Assistant:

Let us give thanks to God the Fa - ther,

al - ways and for ev - 'ry thing.

All:

In the name of our Lord Je - sus Christ.

Assistant:

We praise you, O Lord our God,

Rul - er of the un - i - verse!

Your word brings on the dusk of eve - ning,

your wis - dom cre - ates both night and day.

You de - ter - mine the cy - cles of time,

ar - range the suc - ces - sion of sea - sons,

and es - tab - lish the stars in their heaven-ly cour - ses.

Lord of the star - ry hosts is your name.

Liv - ing and e - ter - nal God,

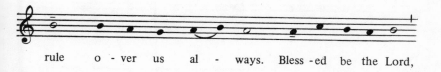

rule o - ver us al - ways. Bless -ed be the Lord,

All:

whose word makes eve - ning fall. A - men.

Thanksgiving (Ordinary Time)

J.A.M.
P.T.L.

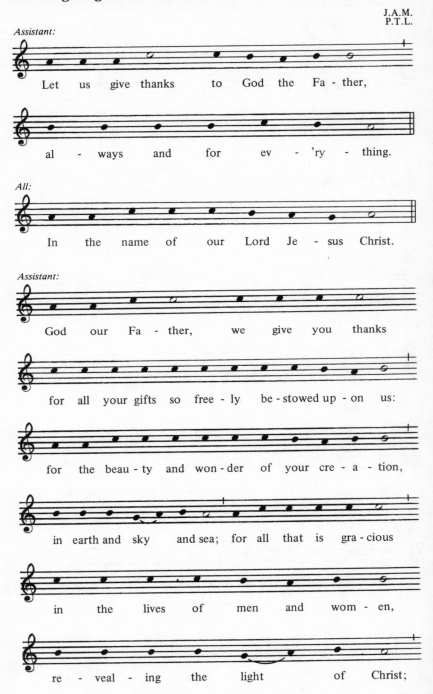

Assistant:

Let us give thanks to God the Fa - ther,

al - ways and for ev - 'ry - thing.

All:

In the name of our Lord Je - sus Christ.

Assistant:

God our Fa - ther, we give you thanks

for all your gifts so free - ly be - stowed up - on us:

for the beau - ty and won - der of your cre - a - tion,

in earth and sky and sea; for all that is gra - cious

in the lives of men and wom - en,

re - veal - ing the light of Christ;

226

for minds to muse and hearts to love and hands to serve;

for health and strength to work,

for lei - sure to rest and play;

for com - mun - ion with your saints,

in all times and plac - es;

and a - bove all, for the great prom - is - es and mer - cies

giv - en to us in Christ Je - sus our Lord.

To him be praise and glo - ry,

with you and the Ho - ly Spir - it,

All:

now and for ev - er. A - men.

Thanksgiving (Ordinary Time)

J.A.M.
Apostolic Tradition

Assistant:

Let us give thanks to God the Fa - ther,

al - ways and for ev - 'ry thing.

All:

In the name of our Lord Je - sus Christ.

Assistant:

We praise and thank you, O God,

through your Son Je - sus Christ our Lord,

through whom you have en - light - ened us

by re - veal - ing the light that nev - er fades.

Joy to all crea - tures, hon - or, feast - ing and de - light,

228

Night is fall - ing and day's al - lot - ted span draws to a close.

We have en - joyed your gift of day - light; bright - en now our eve - ning hours.

We praise and glo - ri - fy you, Fa - ther, through your Son, our Lord Je - sus Christ,

All:

in the Ho - ly Spir - it, now and for ev - er. A-men.

Thanksgiving (Advent)

J.A.M.

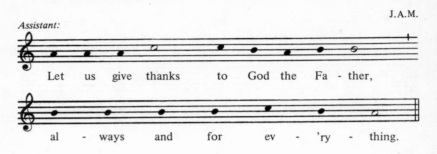

Assistant:

Let us give thanks to God the Fa - ther,

al - ways and for ev - 'ry - thing.

All:

In the name of our Lord Je - sus Christ.

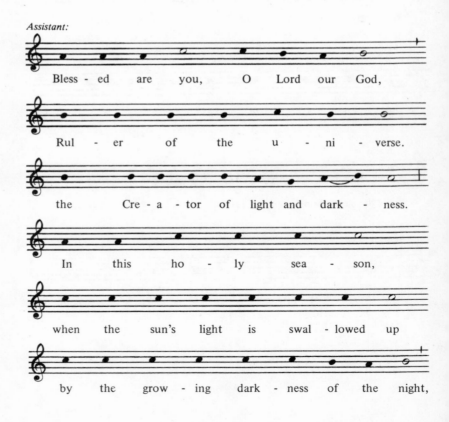

Assistant:

Bless - ed are you, O Lord our God,

Rul - er of the u - ni - verse.

the Cre - a - tor of light and dark - ness.

In this ho - ly sea - son,

when the sun's light is swal - lowed up

by the grow - ing dark - ness of the night,

230

you re - new your prom-ise to re - veal a - mong us

the splen - dor of your glo - ry,

en - fleshed and vis - i - ble to us

in Je - sus Christ, your Son. Through the

proph - ets you teach us to hope for his reign of peace.

Through the out - pour - ing of his Spir - it,

you o - pen our blind - ness to the glo - ry

of his pres - ence. Strength-en us in our weak-ness.

Sup - port us in our stum - bling ef - forts

to do your will and free our tongues

All:

to sing your praise. For to you all hon - or

and bless - ing are due, now and for - ev - er. A-men.

231

Thanksgiving (Christmas)

J.A.M.

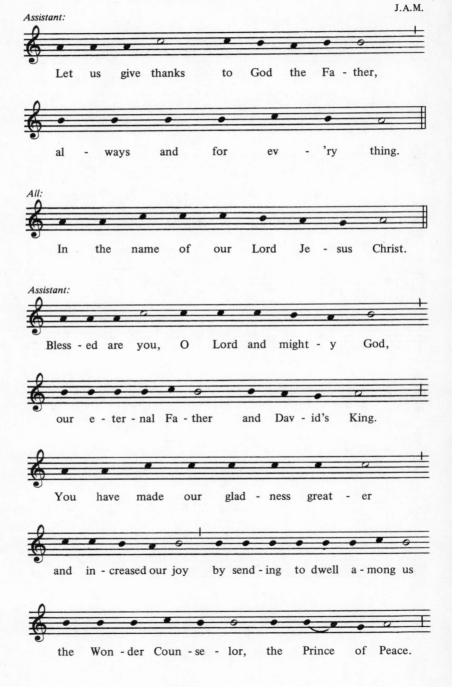

Assistant:

Let us give thanks to God the Fa - ther,

al - ways and for ev - 'ry thing.

All:

In the name of our Lord Je - sus Christ.

Assistant:

Bless - ed are you, O Lord and might - y God,

our e - ter - nal Fa - ther and Dav - id's King.

You have made our glad - ness great - er

and in - creased our joy by send - ing to dwell a - mong us

the Won - der Coun - se - lor, the Prince of Peace.

Born of Mar - y, pro - claimed to the shep - herds

and ac - know - edged to the ends of the earth,

your un - con - quered Sun of Jus - tice

des - troys our dark - ness and es - tab - lish - es us in free - dom

and we are led forth from bond - age.

All glo - ry in the high - est be to you,

through Christ, the Son of your fav - or,

in the a - noint - ing love of his Spir - it

All:

this night and for ev - er and ev - er. A - men.

Thanksgiving (Lent)

J.A.M.

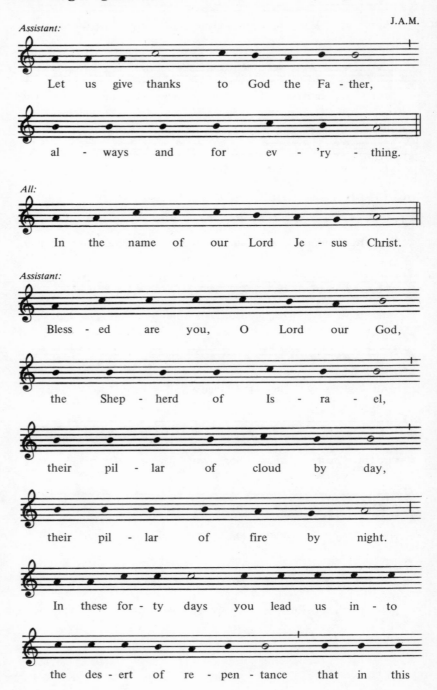

Assistant:

Let us give thanks to God the Fa - ther,

al - ways and for ev - 'ry - thing.

All:

In the name of our Lord Je - sus Christ.

Assistant:

Bless - ed are you, O Lord our God,

the Shep - herd of Is - ra - el,

their pil - lar of cloud by day,

their pil - lar of fire by night.

In these for - ty days you lead us in - to

the des - ert of re - pen - tance that in this

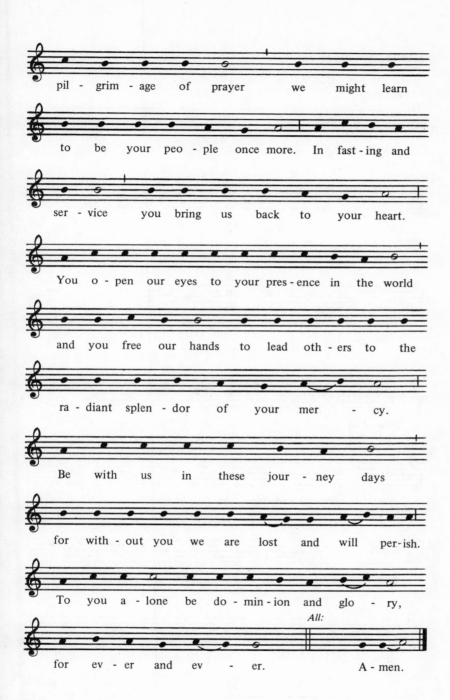

pil - grim - age of prayer we might learn
to be your peo - ple once more. In fast - ing and
ser - vice you bring us back to your heart.
You o - pen our eyes to your pres - ence in the world
and you free our hands to lead oth - ers to the
ra - diant splen - dor of your mer - cy.
Be with us in these jour - ney days
for with - out you we are lost and will per - ish.
To you a - lone be do - min - ion and glo - ry,

All:

for ev - er and ev - er. A - men.

Thanksgiving (Easter)

J.A.M.

Assistant:

Let us give thanks to God the Fa - ther,

al - ways and for ev - 'ry - thing.

All:

In the name of our Lord Je - sus Christ.

Assistant:

Bless - ed are you, O Lord Re - deem - er God.

You de - stroyed the bonds of death

and from the dark - ness of the tomb

drew forth the light of the world.

Led through the wa - ters of death,

we be - come the chil - dren of light

sing - ing our Al - le - lu - ia

and danc - ing to the mu - sic of new life.

Pour out your Spir - it up - on us

that dreams and vis - ions bring us ev - er clos - er to the

king - dom of Je - sus Christ, our Ris - en Sav - ior.

Through him and in the Ho - ly Spir - it

all glo - ry be to you, Al - might - y Fa - ther,

All:

this night and for ev - er and ev - er. A - men.

Psalm 140/141: Evening Prayer for Forgiveness and Protection

Antiphon

H.H.

fore you, O Lord, the lift-ing up of my

fore you, O Lord, the lift-ing up of my

hands like an ev'-ning of-fer - ing. Al - le -

hands like an ev'-ning of-fer - ing. Al - le -

lu, Al - le - lu - ia!

lu, Al - le - lu - ia!

239

Verses

Slightly slower than Refrain; with more freedom

1. I have called to you, Lord; has - ten to help me! Hear my voice when I cry to you. Let my pray'r a - rise be - fore you like in - cense, the rais - ing of my hands like an ev' - ning ob - la - tion.

Antiphon

2; Set, O Lord, a guard o - ver my mouth; keep watch at the door of my lips! Do not turn my heart to things that are wrong, to e - vil deeds with those who are sin - ners.

Antiphon

cresc.

cresc.

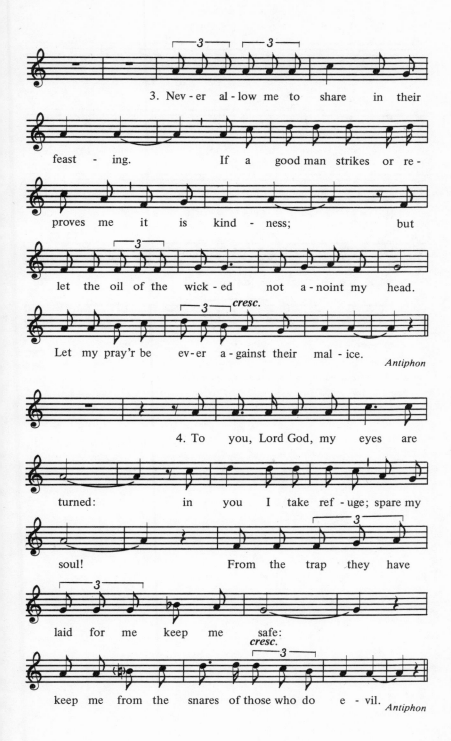

3. Nev-er al-low me to share in their feast - ing. If a good man strikes or re-proves me it is kind - ness; but let the oil of the wick-ed not a-noint my head. Let my pray'r be ev-er a-gainst their mal - ice.

Antiphon

4. To you, Lord God, my eyes are turned: in you I take ref - uge; spare my soul! From the trap they have laid for me keep me safe: keep me from the snares of those who do e - vil.

Antiphon

241

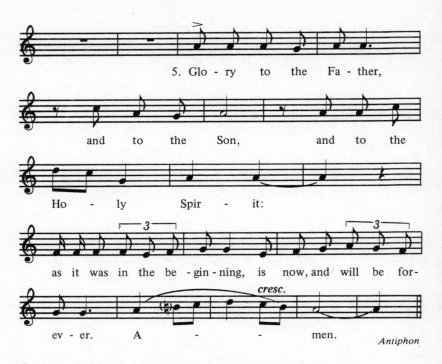

5. Glo - ry to the Fa - ther,

and to the Son, and to the

Ho - ly Spir - it:

as it was in the be - gin - ning, is now, and will be for-

cresc.

ev - er. A - - men.

Antiphon

See the standard forms of Evening Prayer for the appropriate psalm prayer.

242

Psalm 4: An Evening Prayer

G. Weitz

Antiphon

The Lord

The Lord hears my

The Lord

prayer when - ev - er I call.

Verses

J. Gelineau, S.J.

1.   When I   call,   answer   me, O
2.   O   men,   how   long   will   your
3.   It is the   Lord who grants   favours   to
4. Fear him; do not   sin;   ponder   on   your

1. God   of   justice;   from
2. hearts   be   closed,   will   you
3. those whom   he   loves;   the
4. bed   and   be   still,   Make

1. anguish you re - leased me, have mercy   and   hear   me!
2. love what is   futile   and   seek what is   false?
3. Lord   hears me when - ever   I   call   him.
4. justice your   sacri-fice and   trust in the   Lord.

5.   "What can bring us   happiness?"
6.   You have   put in - to my   heart   a
7.   I will   lie   down   in   peace   and
8.   Give   praise   to   the   Father, the

B.F.

244

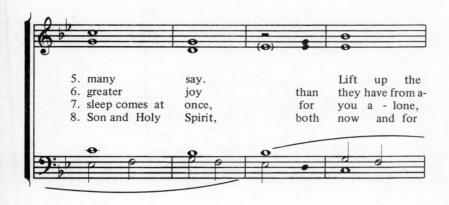

5. many say. Lift up the
6. greater joy than they have from a-
7. sleep comes at once, for you a - lone,
8. Son and Holy Spirit, both now and for

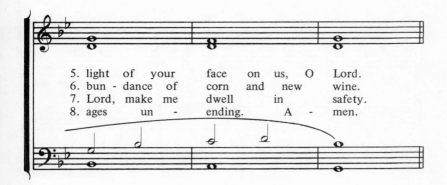

5. light of your face on us, O Lord.
6. bun - dance of corn and new wine.
7. Lord, make me dwell in safety.
8. ages un - ending. A - men.

Psalm Prayer

Leader:

Let us pray. *(Pause for silent prayer.)*

Gracious God,
look on the face of your Christ,
and be our light in the darkness,
our protector as evening falls.
We ask this in Jesus' name.

All:
Amen.

Psalm 22/23: The Lord Jesus, Our Shepherd and Host

Antiphon I My shep-herd is the Lord, noth-ing in-deed shall I want.

J. Gelineau, S.J.

Antiphon II The Lord is my shep - herd,

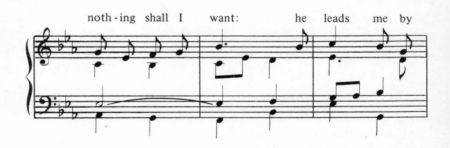

noth-ing shall I want: he leads me by

safe paths, noth - ing shall I fear.

246

A. G. Murray

J. Gelineau, S.J.

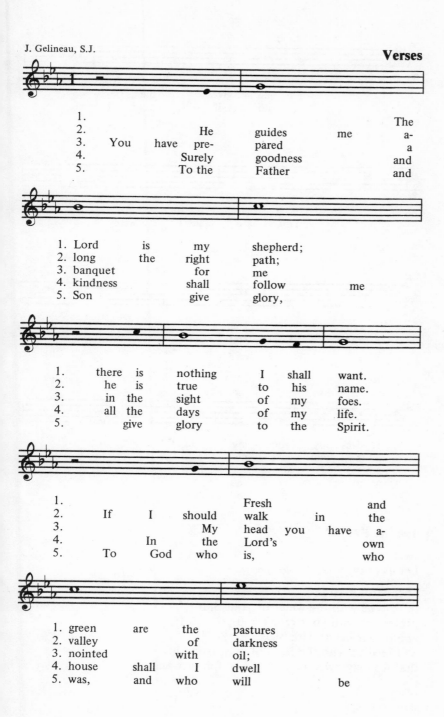

1.
2.   He   guides   me   The
3. You   have   pre-   pared   a-
4.   Surely   goodness   and
5.   To the   Father   and

1. Lord   is   my   shepherd;
2. long   the   right   path;
3. banquet   for   me
4. kindness   shall   follow   me
5. Son   give   glory,

1.   there is   nothing   I   shall   want.
2.   he   is   true   to   his   name.
3.   in the   sight   of   my   foes.
4.   all the   days   of   my   life.
5.   give   glory   to   the   Spirit.

1.   Fresh   and
2. If   I   should   walk   in   the
3.   My   head you have a-
4.   In   the   Lord's   own
5. To   God   who   is,   who

1. green   are   the   pastures
2. valley   of   darkness
3. nointed   with   oil;
4. house   shall   I   dwell
5. was,   and   who   will   be

1. where he gives me re- - pose.
2. no evil would I fear.
3. [
4. [
5. [

1. Near restful
2. You are there with your
3.
4.
5.

1. waters he leads me, to re -
2. crook and your staff; with
3.] my
4.] for
5.] for

1. vive my droop - ing spir - it.
2. these you give me com - fort.
3. cup is o - ver - flow - ing.
4. ev - er and ev - er.
5. ev - er and ev - er.

Psalm Prayer

Leader:

Let us pray. *(Pause for silent prayer.)*

Shepherd of Israel,
refresh us with the water of your Spirit,
protect us with your crook and your staff,
anoint our heads with oil
and feed us with the food of everlasting life
that we may dwell in your house for ever and ever.

All:

Amen.

Psalm 83/84: Yearning for God's Presence

A. G. Murray

(Obligatory before verse 1.) **Antiphon I**

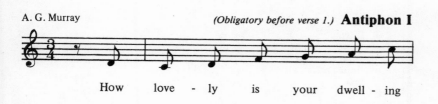

How love - ly is your dwell - ing

place, O Lord of hosts.

J. Geleneau, S.J.

Verses

1.		My	soul	is	longing	and
2.		The	sparrow	her -	self	finds	a
3.	They	are	happy	who	dwell	in	your
4.	As	they	go through the	Bitter		
5.		O	Lord God of	hosts,	hear	my
6.			One	day	with - in	your
7. For	the	Lord	God	is	a	rampart,	a
8.		Give	praise	to the	Father	Al -

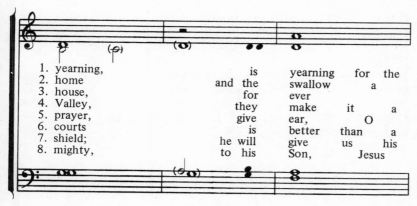

1. yearning,		is	yearning	for the
2. home	and the	swallow	a	
3. house,		for	ever	
4. Valley,	they	make	it	a
5. prayer,	give	ear,	O	
6. courts	is	better	than	a
7. shield;	he will	give	us	his
8. mighty,	to his	Son,	Jesus	

249

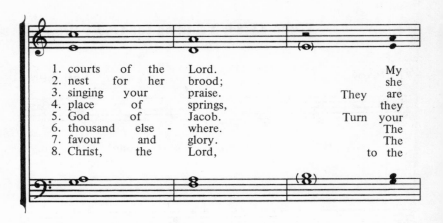

1. courts of the Lord. My
2. nest for her brood; she
3. singing your praise. They are
4. place of springs, they
5. God of Jacob. Turn your
6. thousand else - where. The
7. favour and glory. The
8. Christ, the Lord, to the

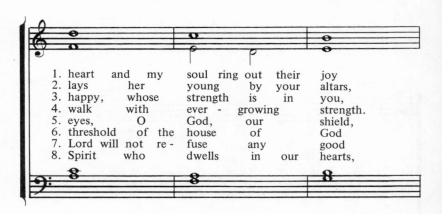

1. heart and my soul ring out their joy
2. lays her young by your altars,
3. happy, whose strength is in you,
4. walk with ever - growing strength.
5. eyes, O God, our shield,
6. threshold of the house of God
7. Lord will not re - fuse any good
8. Spirit who dwells in our hearts,

1. to God, the
2. Lord of hosts, my
3. in whose hearts are the
4. They will see the God of
5. look on the
6. I pre- fer to the
7. to those who
8. both now and for

250

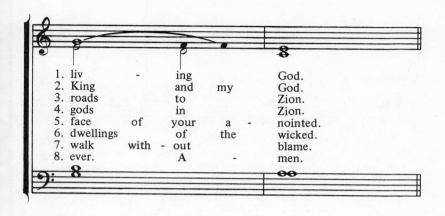

1. liv	-	ing		God.
2. King		and	my	God.
3. roads		to		Zion.
4. gods		in		Zion.
5. face	of	your	a -	nointed.
6. dwellings		of	the	wicked.
7. walk	with -	out		blame.
8. ever.		A	-	men.

(Obligatory after verse 7.) **Antiphon II**

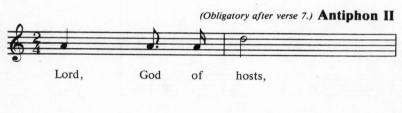

Lord, God of hosts,

hap - py the man who trusts in you.

Psalm Prayer

Leader:

Let us pray. *(Pause for silent prayer.)*

Look on the face of your anointed Son, O Lord,
and by his merits
be to us a rampart and a shield
against the evils of the world
as we pursue our pilgrimage to our heavenly home,
where he reigns with you and the Holy Spirit,
now and for ever.

All:

Amen.

Psalm 133/134: Night Watch

Antiphon

H.H.

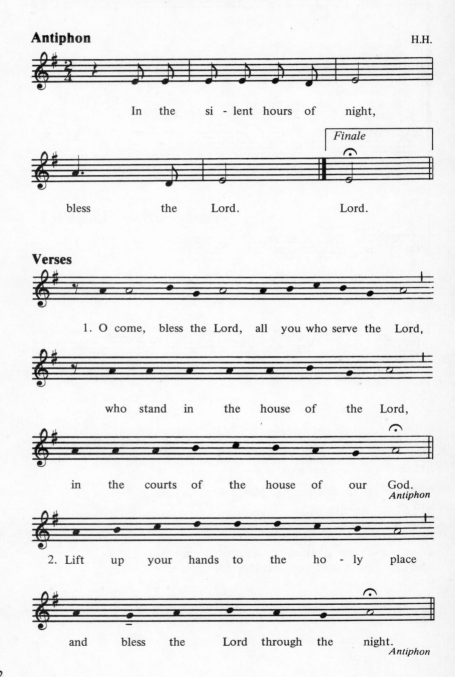

In the si - lent hours of night,

Finale

bless   the   Lord.   Lord.

Verses

1. O come, bless the Lord, all you who serve the Lord,

who stand in the house of the Lord,

in the courts of the house of our God.

Antiphon

2. Lift up your hands to the ho - ly place

and bless the Lord through the night.

Antiphon

3. May the Lord bless you from Zi - on,

he who made both heav - en and earth.
Antiphon

4. Glory to the Father, and to the Son,

and to the Ho - ly Spir - it:

as it was in the be - gin - ning,

is now, and will be for ev - er. A - men.
Antiphon

Psalm Prayer

Leader:

Let us pray. *(Pause for silent prayer.)*

Almighty God,
to whom saints and angels sing,
clothe us in the mantle of praise
that we may rejoice in proclaiming your glory
and in receiving your blessings;
we ask it in Jesus' name.

All:

Amen.

Psalm 135/136: A Hymn of Thanksgiving to our Creator and Savior

Verses

Cantor:

J. Gelineau, S.J.

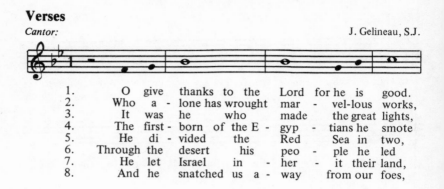

1.   O give thanks to the Lord for he is good.
2. Who a - lone has wrought mar - vel-lous works,
3. It was he who made the great lights,
4. The first - born of the E - gyp - tians he smote
5. He di - vided the Red Sea in two,
6. Through the desert his peo - ple he led
7. He let Israel in - her - it their land,
8. And he snatched us a - way from our foes,

Refrain

All: *f*

Great is his love,   love with - out end.

Cantor: **Verses**

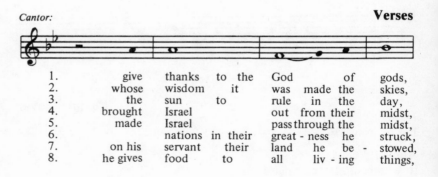

1.   give thanks to the God of gods,
2. whose wisdom it was made the skies,
3. the sun to rule in the day,
4. brought Israel out from their midst,
5. made Israel pass through the midst,
6. nations in their great - ness he struck,
7. on his servant their land he be - stowed,
8. he gives food to all liv - ing things,

All: *f*   **Refrain**

Great is his love,   love with - out end.

Verses

Cantor:

1.	give	thanks	to the Lord	of	Lords.
2.	who	spread	the earth	on the	seas.
3.	the	moon	and stars	in the	night.
4.	arm out -	stretched,	with power	in his	hand.
5.	flung	Pharaoh	and his force	in the	sea.
6.		kings in	their splen - dour he		slew.
7.	he re -	membered	us in	our dis -	tress.
8.	to the	God	of hea - ven give		thanks.

Refrain

All: *f*

Great is his love, love with - out end.

Psalm Prayer

Leader:

Let us pray. *(Pause for silent prayer.)*

Lord Jesus Christ,
you are the bright sun of the universe,
ever rising, never setting;
shine upon our minds
that the night of sin and error
being driven away by your inward light,
we may walk without stumbling, as in the day.
Grant this, O Lord,
you who live and reign
with the Father and the Holy Spirit
now and for ever.

All:

Amen.

Canticle of the Firstborn of All Creation (Col. 1:12-20)

Antiphon

H.H.

To you; O Lord, be hon-or, glo-ry and praise!

Verses

1. Let us give thanks to the Father, for having made us

wor-thy to share the lot of the saints in light.
Antiphon

2. He rescued us from the power of darkness and brought us

into the kingdom of his beloved Son.

Through him we have redemption, the for-giveness of our sins.
Antiphon

3. He is the image of the in-visible God,

the firstborn of all crea-tures.
Antiphon

4. In him everything in heaven and on earth was

cre-at-ed, things visible and in-vis-i-ble,
Antiphon

5. All were created through him, all were created for him.

He is before all else that is. In him everything continues in be-ing.
Antiphon

6. It is he who is head of the body, the church:
he who is the beginning, the firstborn of the dead,
so that primacy may be his in ev-ery-thing.

Antiphon

7. It pleased God to make absolute fullness reside in him
and, by means of him, to reconcile everything in his per-son,
both on earth and in the heavens,
making peace through the blood of his cross.

Antiphon

8. Glory to the Father, and to the Son, and to the Ho-ly Spir-it.
As in the beginning, so now, and for ever. A-men.

Antiphon

Prayer

Leader:

Let us pray. *(Pause for silent prayer.)*

Lord Jesus Christ,
image of the invisible God
and first-born from among the dead,
wash away our sins in your blood
and make us a holy and royal priesthood
to serve your God and Father,
now and for ever.

All:

Amen.

Canticle of the Lamb (Rev. 19:1-7)

Antiphon *with vigor*   H.H.

All   pow'r   is   yours,   Lord God, our might - y

King,   al - le - lu - ia!

Refrain
All:

Al - le - lu - ia,

Al - le - lu - ia!

Verses
Cantor:

1. Salvation, glory   and   power to   our   God:
2. Sing praise to our God   all you his   ser - vants,
3. The Lord our all - powerful   God is   King;
4. The wedding feast of the   Lamb has be -   gun,
5. Glory to the Father, and to the Son,/ and to the Holy Spir - it:

258

Al – le – lu – ia!

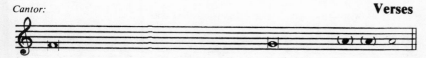

1. his judgments   are   honest and   true.
2. all who worship him reverently,   great and   small.
3. let us rejoice, sing   praise, and give him   glo - ry.
4. and his bride is pre -   pared to   wel-come him.
5. as it was in the beginning, is   ever. A -   men.
   now and will be for

All: **Refrain**

Al – le – lu – ia,

Al – le – lu – ia.

Last time repeat ANTIPHON

Prayer

Leader:

Let us pray. *(Pause for silent prayer.)*

Almighty God and Father,
whose love for us is beyond all description,
prepare us to welcome your Son our Savior
when he comes again in glory
to judge the living and the dead.
He lives and reigns with you and the Holy Spirit,
now and for ever.

All:

Amen.

A Song to the Lamb (Rev. 4:11, 5:9, 10, 12, 13)

Antiphon

H.H.

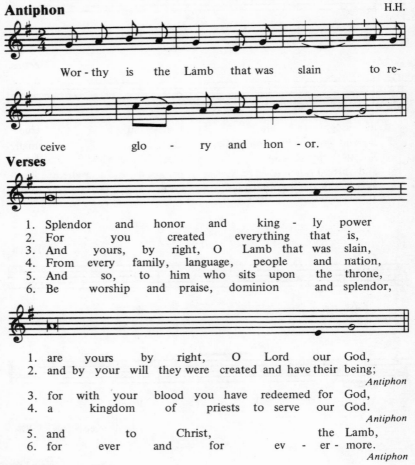

Wor - thy is the Lamb that was slain to re- ceive glo - ry and hon - or.

Verses

1. Splendor and honor and king - ly power
2. For you created everything that is,
3. And yours, by right, O Lamb that was slain,
4. From every family, language, people and nation,
5. And so, to him who sits upon the throne,
6. Be worship and praise, dominion and splendor,

1. are yours by right, O Lord our God,
2. and by your will they were created and have their being;

Antiphon

3. for with your blood you have redeemed for God,
4. a kingdom of priests to serve our God.

Antiphon

5. and to Christ, the Lamb,
6. for ever and for ev - er - more.

Antiphon

Prayer

Leader:

Let us pray. *(Pause for silent prayer.)*

God of peace,
you brought our Lord Jesus Christ back from the dead
and made him the great Shepherd of the sheep
by the blood that sealed an eternal covenant;
make us ready to do your will in all things
and convert us into whatever is acceptable to you;
through the same Christ our Lord.

All:

Amen.

Canticle of Mary (Lk. 1:46-55)

D.C.I.

Antiphon I

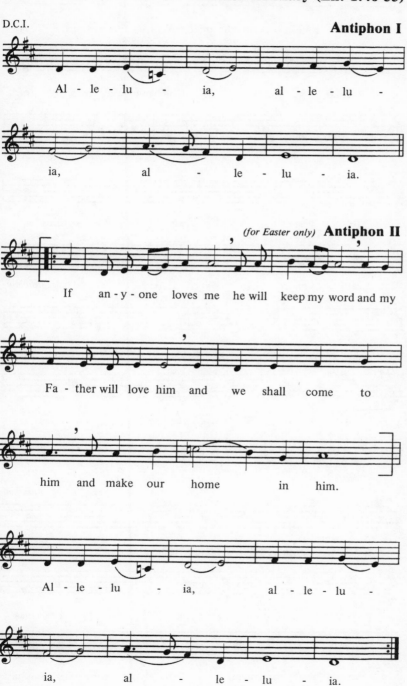

Al - le - lu - ia, al - le - lu -
ia, al - le - lu - ia.

(for Easter only) **Antiphon II**

If an - y - one loves me he will keep my word and my
Fa - ther will love him and we shall come to
him and make our home in him.

Al - le - lu - ia, al - le - lu -
ia, al - le - lu - ia.

261

1. My soul pro-claims the great-ness of the Lord, my
spir-it re-joic-es in God my Sav-ior; for
he has looked with fa-vor on his low-ly ser-vant, and
from this day all gen-er-a-tions will
call me bless - ed. *Antiphon*

2. The Al - might-y has done great things for me, and
Ho-ly is his Name. He has mer-cy on those who
fear him in ev-'ry gen-er-a-tion. *Antiphon*

3. He has shown the strength of his arm, he has
scat-tered the proud in their con-ceit. He has
cast down the might-y from their thrones, and has

262

lift - ed up the low - ly. He has

filled the hun - gry with good things, and the

rich he has sent a - way emp - ty. *Antiphon*

4. He has come to the help of his ser - vant Is - ra -

el for he re - mem-bered his prom - ise of

mer - cy, the prom - ise he made to our fa - thers to

A - bra - ham and his chil - dren for ev - er. *Antiphon*

5. Glo - ry to the Fa - ther, and to the Son, and

to the Ho - ly Spir - it: as it

was in the be - gin - ning, is now and will be for

ev - er. A - men. *Antiphon*

263

Canticle of Mary (Lk. 1:46-55)

II Festal Tone
J. Gelineau, S.J.

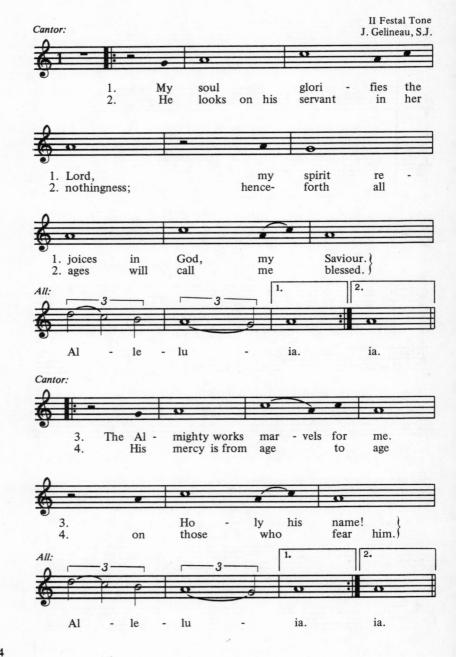

Cantor:

1. My soul glori - fies the
2. He looks on his servant in her

1. Lord, my spirit re -
2. nothingness; hence- forth all

1. joices in God, my Saviour.
2. ages will call me blessed.

All:

Al - le - lu - ia. ia.

Cantor:

3. The Al - mighty works mar - vels for me.
4. His mercy is from age to age

3. Ho - ly his name!
4. on those who fear him.

All:

Al - le - lu - ia. ia.

264

Cantor:

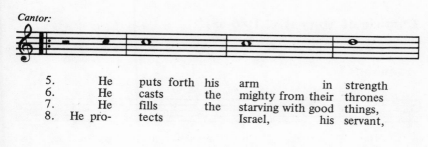

5.	He	puts forth his	arm		in	strength
6.	He	casts	the	mighty from their		thrones
7.	He	fills	the	starving with good		things,
8.	He pro-	tects		Israel,	his	servant,

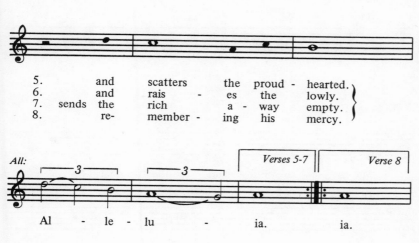

5.		and	scatters	the	proud - hearted.
6.		and	rais - es	the	lowly.
7.	sends	the	rich	a - way	empty.
8.		re-	member - ing	his	mercy.

All:

Verses 5-7 | Verse 8

Al - le - lu - ia. ia.

Cantor:

9.		the	mercy	promised to our	fathers,
10.	Praise the		Father, the	Son and Ho-ly	Spirit,

9.	for	Abra -	ham and his	sons	for
10.	both	now and for	ever,	world	without

All:

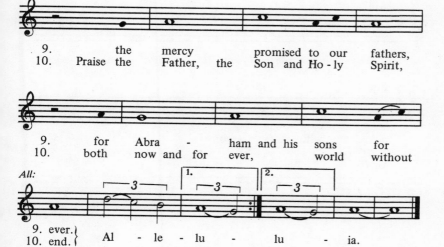

9. ever.
10. end.

Al - le - lu - lu - ia.

Canticle of Mary (Lk. 1:46-55)

Antiphon

D.C.I.

The Al - might - y has done great things for me and

ho - ly, ho - ly, is his name.

Verses

1. My soul pro - claims the great - ness of the

Lord, my spir - it re - joic - es in

God my Sav - iour. For he has

looked with fa - vor on his

low - ly ser - vant. *Antiphon*

2. From this day all gen - er - a -

266

tions will call me bless - ed.

The Al - might - y has done great

things for me and ho - ly,

ho - ly is his Name. *Antiphon*

3. He has mer - cy on those who fear

him in ev - 'ry gen - er - a - tion.

He has shown the strength, the

strength of his arm, he has scat - tered,

267

scat - tered the proud in their con - ceit. *Antiphon*

4. He has cast down the might - y from their

thrones, and has lift - ed up the low - ly.

He has filled the hun - gry with good

things, and the rich he has sent a - way

emp - ty. *Antiphon*

5. He has come to the help of his ser - vant Is - ra-

el, for he has re - mem-bered his pro - mise of

mer - cy,   the   prom - ise he   made to   our

fath   -   ers   to   Ab - ra - ham and   his

chil   -   dren for - ev   -   er.   *Antiphon*

6. Glo - ry   to   the   Fa - ther,   and   to   the

Son,   and   to   the   Ho   -   ly   Spir - it;

as   it   was   in   the   be -

gin   -   ning,   is   now,   and   will

be   for   ev   -   er   A   -   men.
                                                     Antiphon

Canticle of Simeon (Lk. 2:29-32)

M.J.
L. Tibesar

1. Lord, keep our dai - ly course from tears, Safe -
2. Dis - miss your ser - vant now in peace, My
3. Praise Fa - ther, Son, and Spir - it blest, Whose

1. guard us from night's dark - est fears, That,
2. eyes have seen your sav - ing light: A
3. sav - ing works and words at - test To

1. now with Christ, our watch not cease, Un -
2. bright - ness show - ing all the earth The
3. love that passed through death's great strife: Our

270

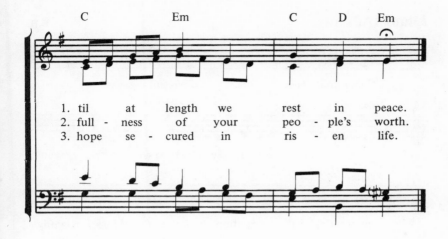

	C		Em		C	D	Em

1. til   at   length   we   rest   in   peace.
2. full - ness   of   your   peo - ple's   worth.
3. hope   se - cured   in   ris - en   life.

Litany

The following could be used in place of the music given in the standard forms of Evening Prayer.

Assistant:

(Petition)   Let   us   pray   to   the   Lord:

All:

Lord,   have   mer - cy,   Lord,   have   mer - cy,

*

Lord,   have   mer - cy.

* This chord may be hummed throughout each following petition.

Litany (Advent)

H.H.

Cantor: Come and save us. *All:* Come and save us.

Cantor: O Wis-dom, breath of the Most High, pervading and permeating all cre-a-tion, ordering all things mightily yet ten-der-ly; come and show us how to live.

All: Come and save us. *Cantor:* O sacred Lord of an-cient Is-ra-el, who appeared to Moses in the burning bush and gave him the law on Si-nai; come, stretch out your mighty hand to set us free.

All: Come and save us. *Cantor:* O Flower of Jes-se's stem, ev-'ry eye is held by you; every prince and

foreign pow-er bows in si-lent wor-ship to your

beau - ty come; let noth - ing keep you from our res - cue.

All: Come and save us. *Cantor:* O Key of Da - vid

and Ruler of the house of Is - ra - el,

controlling at your will the gate of heav - en;

come, break down the pris - on walls of death

and lead your captive nation in - to free - dom.

All: Come and save us. *Cantor:* O Ra - diant Dawn,

splen - dor of e - ter - nal light and sun of jus - tice;

come, shine on those who dwell in dark - ness

and in the shad - ow of death. *All:* Come and save us.

O King of all nations, the only joy of ev-'ry hu-man heart; O Keystone of the might-y arch of time: come and save the crea-ture you fash-ioned from the dust.

All: Come and save us. *Cantor:* O Em-ma-nu-el, God who lives with us to rule and guide, the nations of the earth cry out in long-ing: O come and set us free, our Sav-ior God. *All: allargando* Come and save us.

Concluding Prayer

Leader:
Come, Lord Jesus,
do not delay;
give new courage to your people who trust in your love.
By your coming raise us up to the joy of your kingdom
where you live and reign with the Father and the Holy Spirit,
one God, for ever and ever.

All:
Amen.

Litany (Christmas)

Assistant/Cantor:

Let us complete our evening prayer to the Lord.

All:

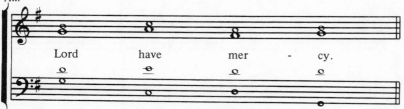

Lord have mer - cy.

By the sacred mysteries of the Word made flesh, let us pray to the Lord.

By the wondrous birth in time of the timeless son of God, let us pray to the Lord.

By the humble nativity of the King of glory in the cave of Bethlehem, let us pray to the Lord.

By the splendid manifestation of the King of the Jews to the shepherds and Magi, let us pray to the Lord.

By the lowly submission of the Maker of the world to Mary and Joseph of Nazareth, let us pray to the Lord.

By the holy baptism of the spotless Son of God by John in the Jordan, let us pray to the Lord.

By the revealing miracle of the water made wine at Cana of Galilee, let us pray to the Lord.

For the conversion of the whole human race to our Lord and Savior Jesus Christ, let us pray to the Lord.

In the communion of the Holy Spirit (and of all the saints), let us commend ourselves and one another to the living God through Christ our Lord.

All:

To you, O Lord.

Concluding Prayer

Leader:

Lord God,
we praise you for creating us,
and still more for restoring us in Christ.
Your Son shared our weakness;
may we share his glory,
for he lives and reigns with you and the Holy Spirit,
one God, for ever and ever.

All:

Amen.

275

Litany (Lent)

Assistant/Cantor:

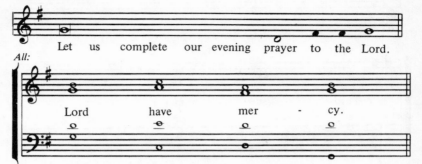

Let us complete our evening prayer to the Lord.

All:

Lord have mer - cy.

For the one, holy, catholic and apostolic Church throughout the world, let us pray to the Lord.

For zealous preachers of the Gospel here and in every land, let us pray to the Lord.

For those preparing for baptism at Easter and for their teachers and sponsors, let us pray to the Lord.

For grace to change our lives according to the pattern of the Gospel, let us pray to the Lord.

For the grace to walk in the footsteps of the saints and to further the reign of God, let us pray to the Lord.

For those who hunger and thirst after justice, freedom and peace, let us pray to the Lord.

For the reconciliation of races, classes and nations in a true human spirit, let us pray to the Lord.

For the sick, the dying and the faithful departed, let us pray to the Lord.

In the communion of the Holy Spirit (and of all the saints), let us commend ourselves and one another to the living God through Christ our Lord.

All:

To you, O Lord.

Concluding Prayer

Leader:

Gracious Father, we pray to you for your holy catholic Church.
Fill it with your truth. Keep it in your peace.
Where it is corrupt, reform it. Where it is in error, correct it.
Where it is right, defend it. Where it is in want, provide for it.
Where it is divided, reunite it;
for the sake of your Son, our Savior Jesus Christ.

All:

Amen.

Litany (Easter)

Assistant/Cantor:

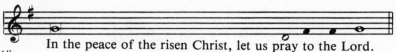

In the peace of the risen Christ, let us pray to the Lord.

All:

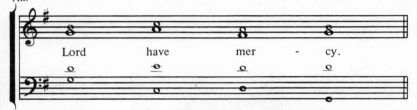

Lord have mer - cy.

That our risen Savior may grant us victory over all our enemies,
seen and unseen, let us pray to the Lord.

That he may crush beneath our feet the prince of darkness and his
powers, let us pray to the Lord.

That he may raise us up with him and set us with him in heaven,
let us pray to the Lord.

That he may fill us with the joy of his holy and life-giving
resurrection, let us pray to the Lord.

That he may provide for those who lack food, work and shelter,
let us pray to the Lord.

That by his power wars and famine may cease through all the earth,
let us pray to the Lord.

That isolated and persecuted churches find fresh strength in the
paschal mysteries, let us pray to the Lord.

That those who have gone before us in the faith of Christ may find
refreshment, light and peace, let us pray to the Lord.

In the communion of the Holy Spirit (and of all the saints), let us
commend ourselves and one another to the living God through
Christ our Lord.

All:

To you, O Lord.

Concluding Prayer

Leader:

God our Father,
by raising Christ your Son
you conquered the power of death
and opened for us the way to eternal life.
Let our paschal celebration
raise us up and renew our lives
by the Spirit that is within us.
You are one God, now and for ever.

All:

Amen.

Resurrection Vigil of the Lord's Day

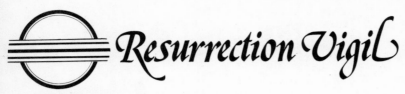

Resurrection Vigil

SERVICE NOTES A night watch, held late on Saturday evening, the Resurrection Vigil is commemorative of the women who brought spices to the tomb early on the first Easter morning. The community gathers in prayer to prepare for the Lord's Day, praising the Father for the resurrection of the Lord.

A chapel, living room or dining room is suitable for the celebration of the Vigil.

In keeping with the spirit of a night watch, those praying may wish to spend some time after the service and before retiring reflecting on the resurrection. The vigil is the introduction to the Day of the Lord and should be the last activity of Saturday. Thus, it is not prayed, except late Saurday night.

Light

The Proclamation, Hymn and Act of Thanksgiving focus on the mystery of resurrection. Praise is offered to the heavenly Father for the gift of Christ Jesus and his Spirit.

The Praises and the Gospel Proclamation

The traditional Easter psalm, Psalm 118, is prayed; either one or both portions of the psalm may be used.

Psalm 150 announces the Gospel Proclamation of the resurrection, the core of the service.

A brief homily or shared reflection may follow a period of silence after the proclamation.

Baptismal Memorial

In families and small groups, the blessing of water may be shortened; if deemed necessary and appropriate, a family may use water already blessed, but the prayer of blessing is highly recommended.

Various forms for the Memorial are suggested, but others may be developed which fit the circumstances of the group at prayer.

The Canticle of Moses or the *Te Deum* should, if at all possible, be sung during the Baptismal Memorial.

On occasion, anointing with fragrant oil may be suitable and replace the water rite. The Blessing of Oil, inlcuded in the Vigil Supplement, is pointed so that it may be sung.

During the Lenten Season, it is possible to use other gestures, such as the imposition of hands, the giving of salted bread, signing of the eyes as ritual responses to the Gospel proclamation. The following model phrases may be used for the various ritual actions.

Water: Be renewed and refreshed by the water of life. May the Lord lead you to the kingdom where there is living water.

Oil: Be anointed with the oil of gladness that you may find strength in the Word of life.

Imposition of Hands: Be renewed in your commitment to the cross which leads to resurrection.

Salted Bread: Be nourished and strengthened in wisdom as you journey to the Easter mysteries.

Signing of the Eyes: May your eyes be opened to the light of the Gospel.

The Acclamations follow the memorial action immediately.

Blessing

A Blessing concludes the service. Exchanging the Sign of Peace may follow.

Resurrection Vigil

MUSICAL SETTING: HOWARD HUGHES, SM

LIGHT Proclamation

All stand *The room is dimly lit. We give praise to Christ, the true light of the world. The assistant lights the paschal candle or another suitable candle and proclaims:*

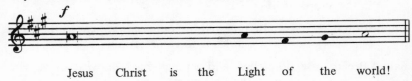

Jesus Christ is the Light of the world!

All respond:

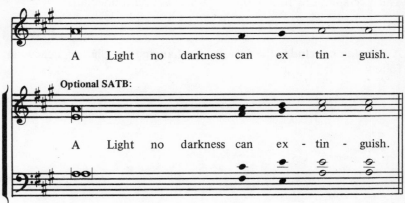

A Light no darkness can ex-tin-guish.

Optional SATB:

A Light no darkness can ex-tin-guish.

282

Hymn

As the lights are lit, the hymn is sung. If the setting permits, the paschal candle is incensed by the assistant.

O Light Serene

(♩. = c. 60)

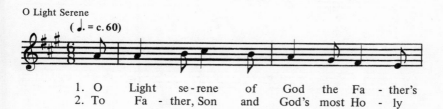

1. O Light se - rene of God the Fa - ther's
2. To Fa - ther, Son and God's most Ho - ly

1. glo - ry, To you, O Christ, we
2. Spir - it, E - ter - nal praise is

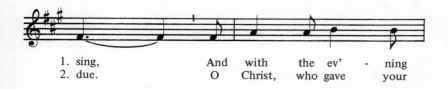

1. sing, And with the ev' - ning
2. due. O Christ, who gave your

1. star, at hour of sun - set, Our
2. life, the world gives glo - ry And

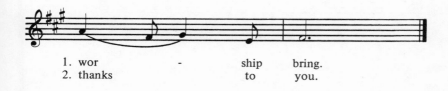

1. wor - ship bring.
2. thanks to you.

Thanksgiving

Assistant:

Let us give thanks to God the Fa - ther,

al - ways and for ev - 'ry thing.

All:

In the name of our Lord Je - sus Christ.

Assistant:

We praise and thank you, O God our Fa - ther,

through your Son, Je - sus Christ our Lord.

Through him you have en - light - ened us

by re - veal - ing the Light that nev - er fades.

for dark death has been de - stroyed

and ra - diant life is re - stored ev - 'ry - where.

What was prom - ised is ful - filled:

we have been joined to God,

through re - newed life in the Spir - it of the Ris - en

Lord. Glo - ry and praise to you, our Fa - ther,

through Je - sus your Son,

who lives and reigns with you and the Spir - it,

in the King - dom of Light e - ter - nal,

All:

for ev - er and ev - er. A - men.

THE PRAISES
AND
THE GOSPEL Psalm 117/118

All are seated *One or both portions of Psalm 117/118 is prayed.*

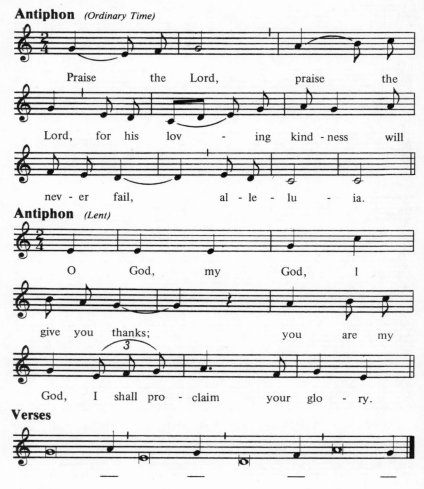

Antiphon *(Ordinary Time)*

Praise the Lord, praise the Lord, for his lov - ing kind - ness will nev - er fail, al - le - lu - ia.

Antiphon *(Lent)*

O God, my God, I give you thanks; you are my God, I shall pro - claim your glo - ry.

Verses

A. *Verses 1-4, 14-21*

1. Give thanks to the Lord for he is good,/ for his love endures for <u>ever</u>.
   Let the sons of Israel say:/ "His love endures for <u>ever</u>.
   Let the sons of Aaron say:/ "His love endures for <u>ever</u>."
   Let those who fear the Lord say:/ "His love endures for <u>ever</u>."

   Antiphon

2. The Lord is my strength and my <u>song</u>;
   He is my <u>savior</u>.
   There are shouts of joy and <u>victory</u>
      in the tents of the <u>just</u>.

286

Antiphon

3. The Lord's right hand has triumphed;/ his right hand <u>raised</u> me.
   The Lord's right hand has triumphed;/
       I shall not die, I shall live and recount his <u>deeds</u>.
   I was punished, I was punished by the <u>Lord</u>, but not doomed to <u>die</u>.
                                                     Antiphon

4. Open to me the gates of holiness:/ I will enter and give <u>thanks</u>.
   This is the Lord's own gate / where the just may <u>enter</u>.
   I will thank you for you have <u>answered</u> and you are my <u>savior</u>.
                                                     Antiphon

(Omit if both portions of the psalm are being used.)

5. Give praise to the Father Al-<u>mighty</u>,
       to his Son, Jesus Christ, the <u>Lord</u>,
       to the Spirit who dwells in our <u>hearts</u>,
       both now and for ever. A-<u>men</u>.
                                                     Antiphon

B. *Verses 22-29*

1. The stone which the builders rejected / has become the <u>corner</u> stone.
   This is the work of the Lord,/ a marvel in our <u>eyes</u>.
   This day was made by the <u>Lord</u>; we rejoice and are <u>glad</u>.
                                                     Antiphon

2. O Lord, grant us salvation;/ O lord, grant suc-<u>cess</u>.
   Blessed in the name of the Lord is he who <u>comes</u>.
   We bless you from the house of the <u>Lord</u>;
       the Lord God is our <u>light</u>.
                                                     Antiphon

3. Go forward in procession with branches even to the <u>altar</u>.
   You are my God, I thank you./ My God, I <u>praise</u> you.
   Give thanks to the Lord for he is <u>good</u>;
       for his love endures for <u>ever</u>.

4. Give praise to the Father Al-<u>mighty</u>,
       to his Son, Jesus Christ, the <u>Lord</u>;
       to the Spirit who dwells in our <u>hearts</u>,
       both now and for ever. A-<u>men</u>.
                                               Antiphon

Psalm Prayer

The leader invites everyone to pray in silence for a moment:
Let us pray.

Then the leader offers the following psalm prayer in the name of the community:
God our Father,
by raising Christ your Son,
you conquered the power of death
and opened for us the way to eternal life.
Let our celebration this night
raise us up and renew our lives
by the Spirit who lives within us.
Grant this through our Lord Jesus Christ, your Son,
who lives and reigns with you and the Holy Spirit,
one God, for ever and ever.

All:
Amen.

Gospel Acclamation

All stand   *As Psalm 150 is sung, there is a procession with the Book of the Gospels, if space permits. Lights and incense may accompany the procession.*

Antiphon *(Ordinary Time)*

Al - le - lu - ia, al - le - lu - ia!

Al - le - lu - ia, al - le - lu - ia!

Antiphon *(Lent)*

Praise God for his might - y deeds.

Verses

1. Praise God in his ho - ly place,
2. O praise him with sound of trum - pet,
3. O praise him with re-sound - ing cym - bals,
4. Give praise to the Fa - ther Al - might - y,

1. praise him in his might - y heav - ens.
2. praise him with lute and harp.
3. praise him with clash - ing of cym - bals.
4. to his Son, Jesus Christ, the Lord,

1. Praise him for his pow-er - ful deeds,
2. Praise him with tim - brel and dance,
3. Let everything that lives and that breathes
4. to the Spirit who dwells in our hearts,

1. praise his sur - pass - ing great - ness.
2. praise him with strings and pipes.
3. give praise to the Lord.
4. both now and for ev - er. A - men.

288

Gospel Proclamation

A Gospel account of the resurrection is proclaimed by an ordained leader or a reader.

When the Sabbath was over,
Mary Magdalene, Mary the mother of James, and Salome
brought perfume oils with which they intended to go and anoint Jesus.
Very early, just after sunrise, on the first day of the week
they came to the tomb.
They were saying to one another,
"Who will roll back the stone for us from the entrance to the tomb?"
When they looked, they found that the stone had been rolled back.
On entering the tomb they saw a young man
sitting at the right, dressed in a white robe.
This frightened them thoroughly, but he reassured them:
"You need not be amazed! You are looking for Jesus of Nazareth,
the one who was crucified.
He has been raised up; he is not here.
See the place where they laid him.
Go now and tell his disciples and Peter,
"He is going ahead of you to Galilee,
where you will see him just as he told you." *(Mark 16:1-7)*

At the end of the reading, the reader raises the Bible and says:
This is the Gospel of the Lord.

All respond:
Praise to you, Lord Jesus Christ.

All pray in silence, opening their minds and hearts to the Spirit.

Other Gospel accounts:

Matthew 28:1-10, 16-20

Mark 16:9-20

Luke 24:1-12

Luke 24:13-35

Luke 24:36-53

John 20:1-10

John 20:11-18

John 20:19-31

John 21:1-14

BAPTISMAL
MEMORIAL The Blessing of the Water

All stand *The water, which stands in a prominent place, is now blessed.*

Leader: *Book of Common Prayer*, 1979

We give you thanks, Al - might - y God,

for the gift of wa - ter. O-ver it the Ho-ly Spir-it moved

in the be-gin - ning of cre - a - tion. Through it you led

the chil - dren of Is - ra - el out of their bond-age.

In it your Son Je - sus re - ceived the bap-tism of John

and was a-noint - ed by the Ho - ly Spir - it

as the Mes - si - ah. We give you thanks,

Fa - ther, for the wa - ter of Bap - tism.

In it we are bur-ied with Christ in his death.

By it we share in his re - sur - rec - tion.

Through it we are re-born by the Ho - ly Spir - it.

Sanc - ti - fy this wa - ter, we pray you,

by the pow - er of your Ho - ly Spir - it

that we may con -tin - ue for ev - er in the ris - en life

of Je - sus Christ our Sav - ior.

To him, to you, and to the Ho - ly Spir - it,

be all hon - or and glo - ry,

All:

now and for ev - er. A - men.

The Baptismal Memorial

According to circumstances, one of the following forms may be used for the memorial of baptism:

- *all approach the blessed water; water is poured by the leader over the extended hands of the person; the individual signs himself or herself with the sign of the cross.*
- *all approach the blessed water; the individual dips his or her hands in the water and signs himself or herself with the sign of the cross.*
- *appropriate branches are dipped in the water and the praying community is generously sprinkled with the blessed water.*

During the ritual action the Song of Moses and Miriam or a New Testament Canticle is sung.

Antiphon

Song of Moses and Miriam
Exodus 15

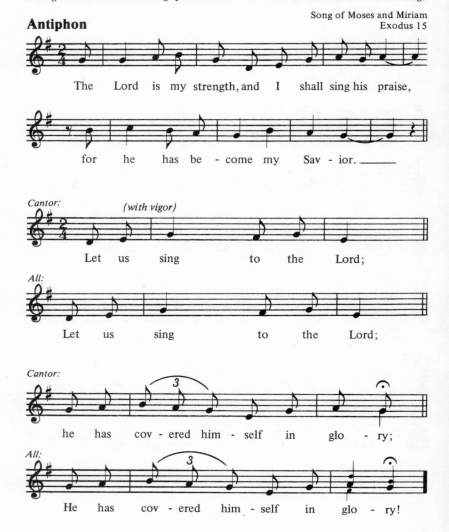

The Lord is my strength, and I shall sing his praise,

for he has be - come my Sav - ior. _____

Cantor: (with vigor)

Let us sing to the Lord;

All:

Let us sing to the Lord;

Cantor:

he has cov - ered him - self in glo - ry;

All:

He has cov - ered him - self in glo - ry!

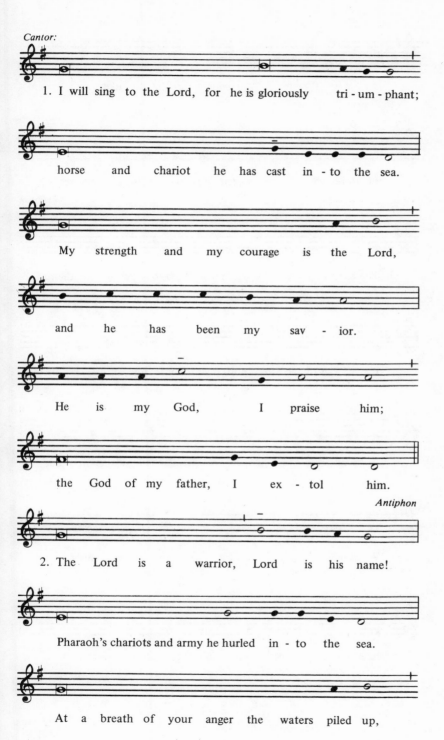

Cantor:

1. I will sing to the Lord, for he is gloriously tri - um - phant;

horse and chariot he has cast in - to the sea.

My strength and my courage is the Lord,

and he has been my sav - ior.

He is my God, I praise him;

the God of my father, I ex - tol him.

Antiphon

2. The Lord is a warrior, Lord is his name!

Pharaoh's chariots and army he hurled in - to the sea.

At a breath of your anger the waters piled up,

293

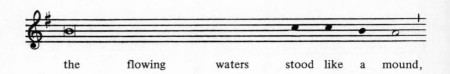

the   flowing   waters   stood like a   mound,

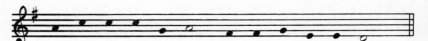

the flood wa - ters con - gealed in the midst of the sea.

Antiphon

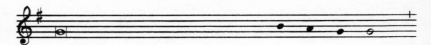

3. The enemy boasted, "I will pursue and o - ver - take them;

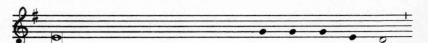

I   will   divide the spoils and have my   fill   of them;

I will draw my sword; my hand shall de - spoil them!

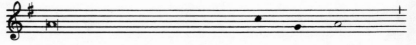

When your wind blew, the   sea cov - ered   them;

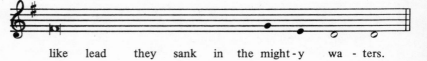

like   lead   they   sank in the might - y wa - ters.

Antiphon

4. Who is like to you among the gods, O Lord?

Who is like to you, mag-ni - fi - cent in ho -li - ness?

O terrible in renown, worker of won - ders,

when you stretched out your right hand,

the earth swal - lowed them!

Antiphon

5. In your mercy you led the people you re - deemed;

in your strength you guided them to your ho - ly dwell - ing.

And you brought them in and planted them on

the mountain of your in - her - i - tance --

the place where you made your seat, O Lord,

the sanctuary, O Lord, which your hands es - tab - lished.

The Lord shall reign for - ev - er and ev - er.

Antiphon

6. Glory to the Father, and to the Son,

and to the Ho - ly Spir - it.

As it was in the be - gin - ning,

is now and will be for ev - er. A - men.

Antiphon

Acclamations

297

Assistant:

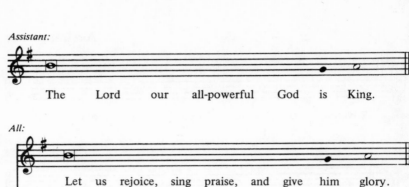

The   Lord   our   all-powerful   God   is   King.

All:

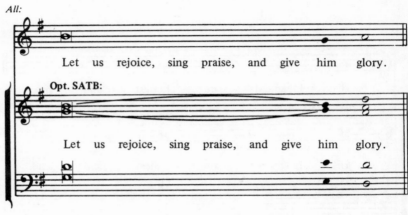

Let   us   rejoice,   sing   praise,   and   give   him   glory.

Opt. SATB:

Let   us   rejoice,   sing   praise,   and   give   him   glory.

Assistant:

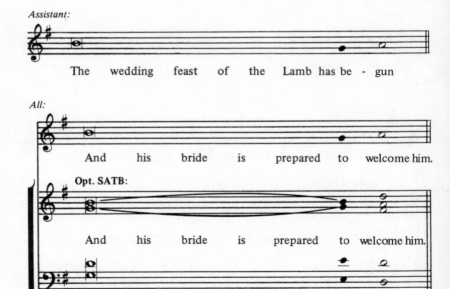

The   wedding   feast   of   the   Lamb has be - gun

All:

And   his   bride   is   prepared   to   welcome him.

Opt. SATB:

And   his   bride   is   prepared   to   welcome him.

Leader:

Lord God, in the new covenant you shed light on the miracles

you worked in an-cient times: the Red Sea is a symbol

of our baptism and the nation you freed from slavery

is a sign of your Chris-tian peo-ple. May every nation

share the faith and privilege of Israel and come to new birth

in the Ho-ly Spir-it. We ask this through Christ our Lord.

All:

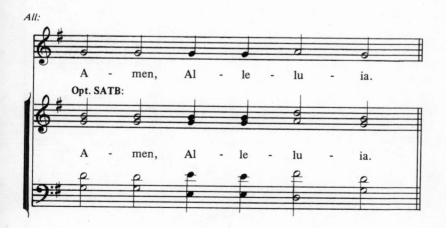

A - men, Al - le - lu - ia.

Opt. SATB:

A - men, Al - le - lu - ia.

BLESSING *Leader:*

May God the Father, who raised Christ Jesus from the dead,

continually show us his lov-ing kind-ness.

All: A - men.

Opt. SATB: A - men.

Leader:

May God the Son, Victor over sin and death, grant us a share

in the joy of his res - ur - rec - tion.

All: A - men.

Opt. SATB: A - men.

Leader:

May God the Spirit, giver of light and peace, renew our

hearts in his love.

All:

A - men.

Opt. SATB

A - men.

Leader:

May almighty God continue to bless us,

the Fa - ther, the Son and the Ho - ly Spir - it.

All:

A - men, Al - le - lu - ia.

Opt. SATB:

A - men, Al - le - lu - ia.

Vigil Supplement

Blessing of Oil

Leader:

Book of Common Prayer, 1979

E - ter - nal Fa - ther, whose bless - ed Son

was a - noint - ed by the Ho - ly Spir - it

to be the Sav - ior and ser - vant of all,

we pray you to sanc - ti - fy this oil

that those who are signed with it may share

in the roy - al priest - hood of love

and ser - vice in Je - sus Christ,

who lives and reigns with you and the Ho - ly

All:

Spir - it, for ev - er and ev - er. A - men.

The Song of Moses and Miriam (Ex. 15)

Gethsemani Abbey

Capo 3 play (C)

The Wedding of the Lamb (Rev. 19:1-7)

Antiphon

The Lord our God reigns, let earth re - joice,

al - le - lu - ia.

Verses

Cantor:

1. Salvation, glory and might be - long to our God,

All:

Al - le - lu - ia!

Cantor:

For his judgments are true and just.

Antiphon

Cantor:

2. Praise our God, all you his ser - vants,

All:

Al - le - lu - ia!

305

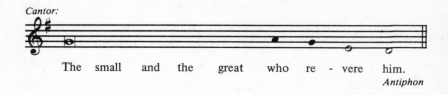

Cantor:

The small and the great who re - vere him.

Antiphon

Cantor:

3. The Lord is king, our God, the Al - might - y,

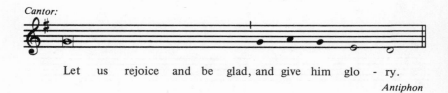

All:

Al - le - lu - ia!

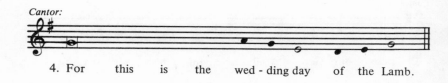

Cantor:

Let us rejoice and be glad, and give him glo - ry.

Antiphon

Cantor:

4. For this is the wed - ding day of the Lamb.

All:

Al - le - lu - ia!

Cantor:

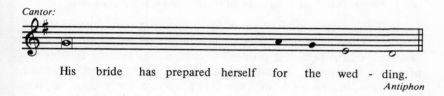

His bride has prepared herself for the wed - ding.

Antiphon

Cantor:

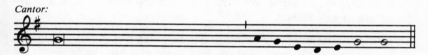

5. Glory to the Father, and to the Son, and to the Ho-ly Spir-it.

All:

Al - le - lu - ia!

Cantor:

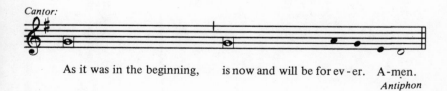

As it was in the beginning, is now and will be for ev-er. A-men.

Antiphon

Other New Testament Canticles may be found in the Evening Supplement.

Appendix

The following tables of hymns, psalms and readings are offered as suggestions for supplementing those included in this volume.

Table 1 contains alternate hymns for daily services. These hymns have been chosen for their distinctly morning or evening character.

Table 2 suggests alternate hymns for use during particular liturgical seasons. They have been selected not only because of the seasonal character of the text, but primarily because they contain themes appropriate to morning or evening. General seasonal hymns have not been included, because they are inappropriate for prayer services which celebrate our union with the Lord throughout the day.

Table 3 is a guide for selecting alternate psalmody in accord with the various seasons. Psalms with morning or evening motifs are appropriate in any season.

Table 4 provides alternate readings for each day of the liturgical year. These Scripture selections, longer than those given in the services, are taken from the Roman Catholic Lectionary for the Liturgy of the Hours.

The following abbreviations will be used in the hymn tables to indicate where the hymns may be found:

BCW   Book of Catholic Worship
The Liturgical Conference
Washington, D.C.
1966

BH   The Book of Hymns
United Methodist Publishing House
Nashville, Tenn.
1964, 1966

CLB   The Catholic Liturgy Book
Helicon Press
Baltimore, Md.
1975

TH   The Hymnal of the Protestant Episcopal Church
in the United States of America   1940
The Church Hymnal Corporation
New York, N.Y.
1940, 1943, 1961

LB   Lutheran Book of Worship
Augsburg, Minn.
1978

LH   The Lutheran Hymnal
Concordia Publishing House
St. Louis, Mo.
1941

MPES   Morning Praise and Evensong
Fides Publications
Notre Dame, Ind.
1973

NCH   New Catholic Hymnal
Faber Music Limited
London, England
1971
(St. Martin's Press, N.Y.)

PMB   Peoples Mass Book
World Library Publications
Chicago, Ill.

W   Worship II
G.I.A. Publications, Inc.
Chicago, Ill.
1975

TABLE 1: Morning
ALTERNATE DAILY HYMNS

All Creatures of Our God and King
2 NCH, 99 BCW, 8 W, 423 CLB, 60 BH,
527 LB

At Thy Feet
498 BH

Awake, My Soul
151 TH, 536 LH, 180 BH, 269 LB

Christ Whose Glory
332 PW, 359 LH, 401 BH, 265 LB, 153 TH

Come, My Soul
337 PW, 154 TH, 359 LH

Come Thou Bright
539 LH

Earth and All Stars
354 PW, 69 W, 558 LB

Every Morning Mercies New
537 LH

Father, We Praise
78 W, 365 PW, 504 BH, 157 TH, 326 CLB,
267 LB

For the Beauty
372 PW, 81 W, 561 LB

God of Our Life
270 LB

God Who Made
549 LH, 281 LB

Holy, Holy, Holy
40 BCW, 421 PW, 266 TH, 246 LH, 26 BH,
91 NCH, 118 W, 165 LB

Immortal, Invisible
135 W, 27 BH, 301 TH, 526 LB

I Sing as I Arise
428 PW

Jesus Shall Reign
472 BH, 530 LB

Joyful, Joyful
154 W, 38 BH, 281 TH, 551 LB

Light of the World
398 BH

Lord, as I Wake (Ps. 5)
135 NCH

Lord of all Hopefulness
144 NCH, 363 TH, 169 W, 469 LB

Lord Jesus, God of Heavenly Grace
135 NCH

Maker of Earth and Heaven
266 LB

Morning Has Broken
159 NCH, 179 W, 323 CLB

New Every Morning
499 BH, 155 TH

Now that the Daylight
325 CLB, 159 TH, 268 LB

Now the Shades
538 LH

O Christ Our True and Only Light
512 LH

O Lord, Our Lord (Ps. 8)
515 PW

O Sing a New Song
525 PW

O Splendor of God's Glory
529 PW, 29 BH, 158 TH, 550 LH

Praise My Soul
72 BCW, 193 NCH, 282 TH, 551 PW,
66 BH, 228 W, 183 PMB, 549 LB

Praise the Lord, His Glories Show
552 PW

Praise the Lord of Heaven (Ps. 148)
424 CLB, 180 PMB, 541 LB

Praise the Lord, Ye Heavens
10 BCW, 194 NCH, 554 PW, 229 W, 540 **LB**

Rise to Greet the Sun
490 BH

See the Morning Sun
7 BH

Sing All Creation (Ps. 100)
589 CLB

The Morning Sun
545 LH

The Radiant Sun
547 LH

The Sun Arises Now
542 LH

This Day God Gives Me
324 CLB

Thy Strong Word
280 W, 233 LB

To God with Gladness Sing
576 CLB

We Lift Our Hearts
492 BH

When Morning Fills the Sky
637 PW, 91 BH, 367 TH, 469 CLB,
545-546 LB

Evening

Abide With Me
278 PW, 289 BH, 552 LH, 493 CLB,
67 TH, 272 LB

All Praise to Thee
292 PW, 493 BH, 165 TH, 16 W, 278 LB
493 BH

Before the Ending
327 CLB, 277 LB

Day is Done
330 CLB

Day is Dying
503 BH

God of All Grace
180 TH

God that Madest Earth
497 BH, 169 TH

God Who Made
404 PW, 281 LB

Heaven and Earth
415 PW

I To the Hills (Ps. 120)
430 PW

Lord Jesus Christ Abide
594 CLB

Now It Is Evening
328 CLB, 167 TH

Now on Land
188 W, 505 BH

Now Rest
554 LH, 282 LB

Now the Day Is Over
172 TH, 495 BH, 330 CLB, 280 LB

O Blest Creator of the Light
163 TH

O Brightness
173 TH

O Christ Who Art
559 LH, 273 LB

O Gladsome Light
197 W, 494 PW, 101 LH, 176 TH, 279 LB

O God Our Help
28 BH, 421 CLB, 203 W, 55 BCW, 594 PW,
123 LH, 289 TH, 179 NCH, 320 LB

O Trinity of Blessed Light
171 TH, 564 LH, 275 LB

Our Day of Praise
175 TH

Softly Now the Light
494 BH, 177 TH

Te Lucis (To You Before the Close of Day)
164 TH, 277 LB

The Day is Past
491 BH

The Day Thou Gavest
500 BH, 179 TH, 263 W, 226 NCH, 274 LB

The Duteous Day
181 TH, 276 LB

The Night is Come
239 NCH

The Setting Sun
242 NCH

The Sun is Sinking
183 TH

The World, My God
520 NCH

Thou Whose Almighty Word
279 W, 272 TH, 508 LH

Unto the Hills (Ps. 120)
57 BH, 445 LB

When Evening Comes
583 CLB

TABLE 2: ALTERNATE SEASONAL HYMNS

Advent

Christ is the World's True Light
60 BCW, 326 PW, 408 BH, 258 TH

Rejoice, Rejoice, Believers
4 TH, 25 LB

The King Shall Come
269 W, 124 MPES, 353 BH, 201 CLB,
11 TH, 33 LB

Wake, Awake
258 NCH, 614 PW, 91 BCW, 291 W,
3 TH, 31 LB

Creator Alme Siderum
348 PW, 120 MPES, 200 CLB, 6 TH,
65 W, 323 LB

Christmas

Christians, Awake
215 CLB, 84 LH

Glorious the Day
91 W

How Brightly (O Morning Star)
119 W, 94 NCH, 343 LH, 443 CLB,
329 TH, 76 LB

Of the Father's Love
219 W, 66 NCH, 66 BCW, 534 PW,
357 BH, 98 LH, 442 CLB, 20 TH, 42 LB

Songs of Praise
214 NCH

Savior of the Nations
241 W, 95 LH, 28 LB

The People Who in Darkness
127 MPES, 361 BH, 106 TH, 6 NCH

Epiphany

Arise and Shine in Splendor
236 CLB, 126 LH

Earth Has Many a Noble City
48 TH, 233 CLB, 70 W, 405 BH, 81 LB

Light of the World
398 BH

Rise, O Light
235 CLB, 138 LH

Thy Strong Word
280 W, 233 LB

The People Who in Darkness
127 MPES, 361 BH, 106 TH, 6 NCH

Saw You Never
50 TH

Lent

O Sun of Justice
245 CLB

From the Deep (Out of the Depths)
(Ps. 129/130)
251 CLB, 295 LB

Sunset to Sunrise
81 TH

When from the Darkness
272 NCH

312

Easter

All Creatures of Our God and King
8 W, 423 CLB, 2 NCH, 99 BCW, 527 LB

Alleluia, Alleluia (Ps. 150)
18 W

At the Lamb's High Feast
89 TH, 275 CLB, 29 W, 81 BCW, 18 NCH,
210 LB

Christ Jesus Lay in Death's Strong Bands
195 LH, 438 BH, 282 CLB, 45 W, 33 NCH,
327 PW, 134 LB

Come, Ye Faithful
58 W, 341 PW, 276 CLB, 204 LH, 448 BH,
94 TH, 132 LB

Hail Thee, Festival Day
86 TH, 109 W, 142 LB

On this Day (also for Sundays)
219 W, 186 NCH, 67 BCW, 416 CLB,
44 PMB

The Day of Resurrection
225 NCH, 280 CLB, 205 LH, 96 TH, 141 LB

This Day at Thy Creating Word
12 LH (also for Sundays)

This Easter Day
270 CLB, 98 TH

This Is the Day When Light
276 W

Welcome, Happy Morning
202 LH, 87 TH, 153 LB

Daylight Fades
281 CLB

The Day of God Destroys the Night
284 CLB

Pentecost

Holy Ghost with Light Divine
234 LH

Come, Gracious Spirit
293 CLB, 475 LB

Come, O Come
338 PW

Hail Thee, Festival Day
86 TH, 109 W, 142 LB

Hail this Joyful Day's Return
295 CLB

Holy Spirit, God of Light
93 NCH, 294 CLB

O Day Full of Grace
161 LB

The Spirit Breathes
243 NCH

313

TABLE 3: ALTERNATE PSALMODY		Morning	Evening
	General	5 8 23/24 28/29 32/33 41/42 46/47 64/65 65/66 91/92 94/95 95/96 97/98 98/99 107/108 134/135 148/150	4 22/23 83/84 90/91 122/123 129/130 130/131 133/134 135/136 137/138 138/139 144/145
	Advent	47/48 65/66 66/67 79/80 84/85	120/121 121/122 122/123 123/124 124/125
	Christmas/ Epiphany	2 45/46 46/47 47/48 71/72	26/27 92/93 95/96 103/104
	Lent	5 31/32 42/43 89/90	18b/19b 35/36 69/70 76b/77b 115/116 136/137
	Easter/ Pentecost	23/24 95/96 96/97 97/98 99/100 134/135	26/27 92/93 116/117 117/118 134/135

	Year 1	Year 2	
Sunday	Is 6:1-13	Is 1:1-18	Week I
Monday	Is 7:1-17	Is 1:21-2:5	
Tuesday	Is 8:1-18	Is 2:6-22; 4:2-6	
Wednesday	Is 9:1b-7	Is 5:1-7	
Thursday	Is 10:5-21	Is 16:1-5; 17:4-8	
Friday	Is 11:10-16	Is 19:16-25	
Saturday	Is 13:1-22a	Is 21:6-12	
Sunday	Is 14:1-21	Is 22:8b-23	Week II
Monday	Is 34:1-17	Is 24:1-18a	
Tuesday	Is 35:1-10	Is 24:18b-25:5	
Wednesday	Ruth 1:1-22	Is 25:6-26:6	
Thursday	Ruth 2:1-13	Is 26:7-21	
Friday	Ruth 2:14-23	Is 27:1-13	
Saturday	Ruth 3:1-18	Is 29:1-8	
Sunday	Ruth 4:1-22	Is 29:13-24	Week III
Monday	1 Chr 17:1-15	Is 30:18-26	
Tuesday	Mic 4:1-7	Is 30:27-31:9	
Wednesday	Mic 5:1-8	Is 32:1-8	
Thursday	Mic 7:7-13	Is 32:9-33:6	
Friday	Mic 7:14-20	Is 33:7-24	
			FROM 17-24
Dec. 17	Is 40:1-11	Is 45:1-13	**DECEMBER**
Dec. 18	Is 40:12-18, 21-31	Is 46:1-13	
Dec. 19	Is 41:8-20	Is 47:1-15	
Dec. 20	Is 41:21-29	Is 48:1-11	
Dec. 21	Is 42:10-25	Is 48:12-21; 49:9b-13	
Dec. 22	Is 43:1-13	Is 49:14-50:1	
Dec. 23	Is 43:19-28	Is 51:1-11	
Dec. 24	Is 44:1-8, 21-23	Is 51:17-52:10	

Christmastide

		Year 1	Year 2
Dec. 25	The Nativity of our Lord		Is 11:1-10
	Sunday within the Octave of Christmas:		
	Feast of the Holy Family		Eph 5:21-6:4
Dec. 26	Stephen the Protomartyr		Acts 6:8-7:2, 44-59
Dec. 27	John, Apostle and Evang.		1 Jn. 1:1-2:3
Dec. 28	The Holy Innocents		Exodus 1:8-16, 22
Dec. 29		Col 1:1-14	S of S 1:1-8
Dec. 30		Col 1:15-2:3	S of S 1:9-2:7
Dec. 31		Col 2:4-15	S of S 2:8-3:5
Jan. 1	Solemnity of Mary Mother of God		Heb 2:9-17
Jan. 2		Col 2:16-3:4	S of S 4:1-5:1

In places where the Epiphany is celebrated on the Sunday occurring between 2-8 January, the readings given for 7-12 January are read after the Epiphany, the following being omitted:

		Year 1	Year 2
Jan. 3		Col 3:5-16	S of S 5:2-6:2
Jan. 4		Col 3:17-4:1	S of S 6:3-7:10
Jan. 5		Col 4:2-18	S of S 7:11-8:7

Jan. 6 *(in places where the Epiphany is celebrated on Jan. 7 or 8)*

| | Is 42:1-8 | Is 49:1-9 |

Jan. 7 *(in places where the Epiphany is celebrated on Jan. 7 or 8)*

| | Is 61:1-11 | Is 54:1-17 |

Jan. 6   The Epiphany of our Lord   Is 60:1-22

The readings assigned to 7-12 January are read on the days which follow the solemnity of the Epiphany, even when this is kept on the Sunday, until the following Saturday. From the Monday after the Sunday on which the Baptism of our Lord is celebrated, i.e. the Sunday occurring after 6 January, the readings of the weeks of the year are begun, omitting any which remain of those assigned to the ferias between 7-12 January.

		Year 1	Year 2
Jan. 7 *or Mon.* *after* Epiphany		Is 61:1-11	Is 54:1-17
Jan. 8 *or Tues.* *after* Epiphany		Is 62:1-12	Is 55:1-13
Jan. 9 *or Wed.* *after* Epiphany		Is 63:7-64:1	Is 56:1-8
Jan. 10 *or Thurs.* *after* Epiphany		Is 64:1-12	Is 59:15-21
Jan 11 *or Fri.* *after* Epiphany		Is 65:13-25	Baruch 4:5-29
Jan 12 *or Sat.* *after* Epiphany		Is 66:5-14a, 18-23	Baruch 4:30-5:9

Sunday after Jan. 6: Feast of the Baptism of our Lord   Is 42:1-8; 49:1-9

Lent

Ash Wednesday Is 58:1-14

	Year 1	Year 2	
Thursday	Deut 1:1, 6-18	Exod 1:1-22	
Friday	Deut 4:1-8, 32-40	Exod 2:1-22	
Saturday	Deut 5:1-22	Exod 3:1-20	
Sunday	Deut 6:4-25	Exod 5:1-6:1	**Week I**
Monday	Deut 7:6-14; 8:1-6	Exod 6:2-13	
Tuesday	Deut 9:7-21, 25-29	Exod 6:29-7:24	
Wednesday	Deut 10:12-11:7, 26-28		
		Exod 10:21-11:10	
Thursday	Deut 12:1-14	Exod 12:1-20	
Friday	Deut 15:1-18	Exod 12:21-36	
Saturday	Deut 16:1-7	Exod 12:37-49; 13:11-16	
Sunday	Deut 18:1-22	Exod 13:17-14:9	**Week II**
Monday	Deut 24:1-25:4	Exod 14:10-31	
Tuesday	Deut 26:1-19	Exod 16:1-18, 35	
Wednesday	Deut 29:2-6, 10-29	Exod 17:1-16	
Thursday	Deut 30:1-20	Exod 18:13-27	
Friday	Deut 31:1-15, 23	Exod 19:1-19; 20:18-21	
Saturday	Deut 32:48-52; 34:1-12		
		Exod 20:1-17	
Sunday	Heb 1:1-2:4	Exod 22:20-23:9	**Week III**
Monday	Heb 2:5-18	Exod 24:1-18	
Tuesday	Heb 3:1-19	Exod 32:1-5, 15-34	
Wednesday	Heb 4:1-13	Exod 33:7-11, 18-23; 34:5-9, 29-35	
Thursday	Heb 4:14-5:10	Exod 34:10-28	
Friday	Heb 5:11-6:8	Exod 35:30-36:1; 37:1-9	
Saturday	Heb 6:9-20	Exod 40:16-38	
Sunday	Heb 7:1-11	Lev 8:1-17; 9:22-24	**Week IV**
Monday	Heb 7:11-28	Lev 16:2-27	
Tuesday	Heb 8:1-13	Lev 19:1-18, 31-37	
Wednesday	Heb 9:1-14	Lev 26:3-17, 38-46	
Thursday	Heb 9:15-28	Num 3:1-13; 8:5-11	
Friday	Heb 10:1-10	Num 9:15-10:10, 33-36	
Saturday	Heb 10:11-25	Num 11:4-6, 10-33	
Sunday	Heb 10:26-39	Num 12:1-15	**Week V**
Monday	Heb 11:1-19	Num 12:16-13:3, 17-33	
Tuesday	Heb 11:20-31	Num 14:1-25	
Wednesday	Heb 11:32-40	Num 16:1-35	
Thursday	Heb 12:1-13	Num 20:1-13; 21:4-9	
Friday	Heb 12:14-29	Num 22:1-8a, 20-35	
Saturday	Heb 13:1-25	Num 24:1-19	

		Year 1	Year 2
Holy Week	Sunday	Is 50:4-51:3	Jer 22:1-8; 23:1-8
	Monday	Is 52:13-53:12	Jer 26:1-15
	Tuesday	Lam 1:1-12, 18-20	Jer 8:13-9:9
	Wednesday	Lam 2:1-10	Jer 11:18-12:13
	Thursday	Lam 2:11-22	Jer 15:10-21
	Friday	Lam 3:1-33	Jer 16:1-15
	Saturday	Lam 5:1-22	Jer 20:7-18

Eastertide

Easter Sunday: Any one of the Vigil readings may be used.

		Year 1	Year 2
Easter Week	Monday	1 Pet 1:1-21	Acts 1:1-26
	Tuesday	1 Pet 1:22-2:10	Acts 2:1-21
	Wednesday	1 Pet 2:11-25	Acts 2:22-41
	Thursday	1 Pet 3:1-17	Acts 2:42-3:11
	Friday	1 Pet 3:18-4:11	Acts 3:12-4:4
	Saturday	1 Pet 4:12-5:14	Acts 4:5-31
Week II	Sunday	Col 3:1-17	Col 3:1-17
	Monday	Rev 1:1-20	Acts 4:32-5:16
	Tuesday	Rev 2:1-11	Acts 5:17-42
	Wednesday	Rev 2:12-29	Acts 6:1-15
	Thursday	Rev 3:1-22	Acts 7:1-16
	Friday	Rev 4:1-11	Acts 7:17-43
	Saturday	Rev 5:1-14	Acs 7:44-8:3
Week III	Sunday	Rev 6:1-17	Acts 8:4-25
	Monday	Rev 7:1-17	Acts 8:26-40
	Tuesday	Rev 8:1-13	Acts 9:1-22
	Wednesday	Rev 9:1-12	Acts 9:23-43
	Thursday	Rev 9:13-21	Acts 10:1-33
	Friday	Rev 10:1-11	Acts 10:34-11:4, 18
	Saturday	Rev 11:1-19	Acts 11:19-30
Week IV	Sunday	Rev 12:1-17	Acts 12:1-23
	Monday	Rev 13:1-18	Acts 12:24-13:14a
	Tuesday	Rev 14:1-13	Acts 13:14b-43
	Wednesday	Rev 14:14-15:4	Acts 13:44-14:7
	Thursday	Rev 15:5-16:21	Acts 14:8-15:4
	Friday	Rev 17:1-18	Acts 15:5-35
	Saturday	Rev 18:1-20	Acts 15:36-16:15
Week V	Sunday	Rev 18:21-19:10	Acts 16:16-40
	Monday	Rev 19:11-21	Acts 17:1-18
	Tuesday	Rev 20:1-15	Acts 17:19-34
	Wednesday	Rev 21:1-8	Acts 18:1-28
	Thursday	Rev 21:9-27	Acts 19:1-20
	Friday	Rev 22:1-9	Acts 19:21-41
	Saturday	Rev 22:10-21	Acts 20:1-16

	Year 1	Year 2	
Sunday	1 Jn 1:1-10	Acts 20:17-38	**Week VI**
Monday	1 Jn 2:1-11	Acts 21:1-26	
Tuesday	1 Jn 2:12-17	Acts 21:27-39	
Wednesday	1 Jn 2:18-29	Acts 21:40-22:21	
Thursday	The Ascension of Our Lord	Eph 4:1-24	
Friday	1 Jn 3:1-10	Acts 22:22-23:11	
Saturday	1 Jn 3:11-17	Acts 23:12-35	
Sunday	1 Jn 3:18-24	Acts 24:1-27	**Week VII**
Monday	1 Jn 4:1-10	Acts 25:1-27	
Tuesday	1 Jn 4:11-21	Acts 26:1-32	
Wednesday	1 Jn 5:1-12	Acts 27:1-20	
Thursday	1 Jn 5:13-21	Acts 27:21-44	
Friday	2 Jn	Acts 28:1-14	
Saturday	3 Jn	Acts 28:15-31	
Pentecost Sunday	Rom 8:5-27		

Ordinary Time

	Year 1	Year 2	
Monday	Rom 1:1-17	Gen 1:1-2:4a	**Week I**
Tuesday	Rom 1:18-32	Gen 2:4b-25	
Wednesday	Rom 2:1-16	Gen 3:1-24	
Thursday	Rom 2:17-29	Gen 4:1-24	
Friday	Rom 3:1-20	Gen 6:5-22; 7:17-24	
Saturday	Rom 3:21-31	Gen 8:1-22	
Sunday	Rom 4:1-25	Gen 9:1-17	**Week II**
Monday	Rom 5:1-11	Gen 11:1-26	
Tuesday	Rom 5:12-21	Gen 12:1-9; 13:2-18	
Wednesday	Rom 6:1-11	Gen 14:1-24	
Thursday	Rom 6:12-23	Gen 15:1-21	
Friday	Rom 7:1-13	Gen 16:1-16	
Saturday	Rom 7:14-25	Gen 17:1-27	
Sunday	Rom 8:1-17	Gen 18:1-33	**Week III**
Monday	Rom 18:18-39	Gen 19:1-17, 23-29	
Tuesday	Rom 9:1-18	Gen 21:1-21	
Wednesday	Rom 9:19-33	Gen 22:1-19	
Thursday	Rom 10:1-21	Gen 24:1-27	
Friday	Rom 11:1-12	Gen 24:33-41, 49-67	
Saturday	Rom 11:13-24	Gen 25:7-11, 19-34	
Sunday	Rom 11:25-36	Gen 27:1-29	**Week IV**
Monday	Rom 12:1-21	Gen 27:30-45	
Tuesday	Rom 13:1-14	Gen 28:10-29:14	
Wednesday	Rom 14:1-23	Gen 31:1-21	
Thursday	Rom 15:1-13	Gen 32:3-30	
Friday	Rom 15:14-33	Gen 35:1-29	
Saturday	Rom 16:1-27	Gen 37:2-4, 12-36	

		Year 1	Year 2
Week V	Sunday	1 Cor 1:1-17	Gen 39:1-23
	Monday	1 Cor 1:18-31	Gen 41:1-15, 25-43
	Tuesday	1 Cor 2:1-16	Gen 41:55-42:26
	Wednesday	1 Cor 3:1-23	Gen 43:1-17, 26-34
	Thursday	1 Cor 4:1-21	Gen 44:1-20, 30-34
	Friday	1 Cor 5:1-13	Gen 45:1-15, 21b-28; 46:1-7
	Saturday	1 Cor 6:1-11	Gen 49:1-28, 33
Week VI	Sunday	1 Cor 6:12-29	1 Thess 1:1-2:12
	Monday	1 Cor 7:1-24	1 Thess 2:13-3:13
	Tuesday	1 Cor 7:25-40	1 Thess 4:1-18
	Wednesday	1 Cor 8:1-13	1 Thess 5:1-28
	Thursday	1 Cor 9:1-18	2 Thess 1:1-12
	Friday	1 Cor 9:19-27	2 Thess 2:1-17
	Saturday	1 Cor 10:1-14	2 Thess 3:1-18
Week VII	Sunday	1 Cor 10:14-11:1	2 Cor 1:1-14
	Monday	1 Cor 11:2-16	2 Cor 1:15-2:11
	Tuesday	1 Cor 11:17-34	2 Cor 2:12-3:6
	Wednesday	1 Cor 12:1-11	2 Cor 3:7-4:4
	Thursday	1 Cor 12:12-31	2 Cor 4:5-18
	Friday	1 Cor 12:31-13:13	2 Cor 5:1-21
	Saturday	1 Cor 14:1-19	2 Cor 6:1-7:1
Week VIII	Sunday	1 Cor 14:20-40	2 Cor 7:2-16
	Monday	1 Cor 15:1-19	2 Cor 8:1-24
	Tuesday	1 Cor 15:20-34	2 Cor 9:1-15
	Wednesday	1 Cor 15:35-58	2 Cor 10:1-11:6
	Thursday	1 Cor 16:1-24	2 Cor 11:7-29
	Friday	Jas 1:1-18	2 Cor 11:30-12:13
	Saturday	Jas 1:19-27	2 Cor 12:14-13:14
Week IX	Sunday	Jas 2:1-13	Gal 1:1-12
	Monday	Jas 2:14-26	Gal 1:13-2:10
	Tuesday	Jas 3:1-12	Gal 2:11-3:14
	Wednesday	Jas 3:13-18	Gal 3:15-4:7
	Thursday	Jas 4:1-12	Gal 4:8-5:1a
	Friday	Jas 4:13-5:11	Gal 5:1b-25
	Saturday	Jas 5:12-20	Gal 5:25-6:18
Week X	Sunday	Sir 46:1-10	Phil 1:1-11
	Monday	Josh 1:1-18	Phil 1:12-26
	Tuesday	Josh 2:1-24	Phil 1:27-2:11
	Wednesday	Josh 3:1-17; 4:14-19; 5:10-12	Phil 2:12-30
	Thursday	Josh 5:13-6:21	Phil 3:1-16
	Friday	Josh 7:4-26	Phil 3:17-4:9
	Saturday	Josh 10:1-15	Phil 4:10-23

	Year 1	Year 2	
Sunday	Josh 24:1-7, 13-28	Is 44:12-45:3	**Week XI**
Monday	Judg 2:6-3:4	Ezra 1:1-8; 2:68-3:8	
Tuesday	Judg 4:1-24	Ezra 4:1-5, 24-5:5	
Wednesday	Judg 6:1-6, 11-24	Hag 1:1-2:9	
Thursday	Judg 7:1-8, 16-22a	Hag 2:10-23	
Friday	Judg 8:22-32; 9:1-15	Zech 1:1-21	
Saturday	Judg 11:1-9, 29-40	Zech 2:1-13	
Sunday	Judg 13:1-25	Zech 3:1-4:14	**Week XII**
Monday	Judg 16:4-6, 16-31	Zech 8:1-17, 20-23	
Tuesday	1 Sam 1:1-19	Ezra 6:1-5, 14-22	
Wednesday	1 Sam 1:20-28; 2:11-21	Ezra 7:6-28	
Thursday	1 Sam 2:22-36	Ezra 9:1-9, 15-10:5	
Friday	1 Sam 3:1-21	Neh 1:1-2:8	
Saturday	1 Sam 4:1-18	Neh 2:9-20	
Sunday	1 Sam 5:1,6-6:4	Neh 4:1-23	**Week XIII**
Monday	1 Sam 7:15-8:22	Neh 5:1-19	
Tuesday	1 Sam 9:1-6, 14-10:1	Neh 7:73b-8:18	
Wednesday	1 Sam 11:1-15	Neh 9:1-2, 5-21	
Thursday	1 Sam 12:1-25	Neh 9:22-37	
Friday	1 Sam 15:1-23	Neh 12:27-47	
Saturday	1 Sam 16:1-13	Is 59:1-14	
Sunday	1 Sam 17:1-10, 23b-26, 40-51	Prov 1:1-7, 20-33	**Week XIV**
Monday	1 Sam 17:57-18:9, 20-30	Prov 3:1-20	
Tuesday	1 Sam 19:8-10; 20:1-17	Prov 8:1-5, 12-36	
Wednesday	1 Sam 21:1-9; 22:1-5	Prov 9:1-18	
Thursday	1 Sam 25:14-24, 28-39	Prov 10:6-32	
Friday	1 Sam 26:2-25	Prov 15:8-30; 16:1-9	
Saturday	1 Sam 28:3-25	Prov 31:10-31	
Sunday	1 Sam 31:1-4; 2 Sam 1:1-16	Job 1:1-22	**Week XV**
Monday	2 Sam 2:1-11; 3:1-5	Job 2:1-13	
Tuesday	2 Sam 4:2-5:7	Job 3:1-26	
Wednesday	2 Sam 6:1-23	Job 4:1-21	
Thursday	2 Sam 7:1-25	Job 5:1-27	
Friday	2 Sam 11:1-17, 26-27	Job 6:1-30	
Saturday	2 Sam 12:1-25	Job 7:1-21	

		Year 1	Year2
Week XVI	Sunday	2 Sam 15:7-14, 24-30; 16:5-13	Job 11:1-20
	Monday	2 Sam 18:6-19:4	Job 12:1-25
	Tuesday	2 Sam 24:1-25	Job 13:13-14:6
	Wednesday	1 Chr 22:5-19	Job 18:1-21
	Thursday	1 Kgs 1:11-35; 2:10-12	Job 19:1-29
	Friday	1 Kgs 3:5-28	Job 22:1-30
	Saturday	1 Kgs 8:1-21	Job 23:1-24:12
Week XVII	Sunday	1 Kgs 8:22-34, 54-61	Job 28:1-28
	Monday	1 Kgs 10:1-13	Job 29:1-10; 30:1, 9-23
	Tuesday	1 Kgs 11:1-4, 26-43	Job 31:1-23, 35-37
	Wednesday	1 Kgs 12:1-19	Job 32:1-6; 33:1-22
	Thursday	1 Kgs 12:20-33	Job 38:1-30; 40:1-5
	Friday	1 Kgs 16:29-17:16	Job 40:6-24; 42:1-6
	Saturday	1 Kgs 18:16b-40	Job 42:7-17
Week XVIII	Sunday	1 Kgs 19:1-21	Obad 1-21
	Monday	1 Kgs 21:1-21, 27-29	Joel 1:13-2:11
	Tuesday	1 Kgs 22:1-9, 15-23, 29, 34-38	Joel 2:12-27
	Wednesday	2 Chr 20:1-9, 13-24	Joel 2:28-3:8
	Thursday	2 Kgs 2:1-15	Joel 3:9-21
	Friday	2 Kgs 3:5-27	Mal 1:1-14; 2:13-16
	Saturday	2 Kgs 4:8-37	Mal 3:1-4:6
Week XIX	Sunday	2 Kgs 4:38-44; 6:1-7	Jonah 1:1-17; 2:10
	Monday	2 Kgs 5:1-19a	Jonah 3:1-4:11
	Tuesday	2 Kgs 6:8-23	Zech 9:1-10:2
	Wednesday	2 Kgs 6:24-25, 32-7:16	Zech 10:3-11:3
	Thursday	2 Kgs 9:1-16, 22-27	Zech 11:4-12:8
	Friday	2 Kgs 11:1-21	Zech 12:9-13:9
	Saturday	2 Kgs 13:10-25	Zech 14:1-21
Week XX	Sunday	Eph 1:1-14	Eccles 1:1-18
	Monday	Eph 1:15-23	Eccles 2:1-26
	Tuesday	Eph 2:1-10	Eccles 3:1-22
	Wednesday	Eph 2:11-22	Eccles 5:10-6:8
	Thursday	Eph 3:1-13	Eccles 6:12-7:28
	Friday	Eph 3:14-21	Eccles 8:5-9:10
	Saturday	Eph 4:1-16	Eccles 11:7-12:14

	Year 1	**Year 2**	
Sunday	Eph 4:17-24	Tit 1:1-16	**Week XXI**
Monday	Eph 4:25-5:7	Tit 2:1-3:2	
Tuesday	Eph 5:8-20	Tit 3:3-15	
Wednesday	Eph 5:21-33	1 Tim 1:1-20	
Thursday	Eph 6:1-9	1 Tim 2:1-15	
Friday	Eph 6:10-24	1 Tim 3:1-16	
Saturday	Philem 1-25	1 Tim 4:1-5:2	
Sunday	2 Kgs 14:1-27	1 Tim 5:3-25	**Week XXII**
Monday	Amos 1:1-2:3	1 Tim 6:1-10	
Tuesday	Amos 2:4-16	1 Tim 6:11-21	
Wednesday	Amos 3:1-15	2 Tim 1:1-18	
Thursday	Amos 4:1-13	2 Tim 2:1-21	
Friday	Amos 5:1-17	2 Tim 2:22-3:17	
Saturday	Amos 5:18-6:14	2 Tim 4:1-22	
Sunday	Amos 7:1-17	2 Pet 1:1-11	**Week XXIII**
Monday	Amos 8:1-14	2 Pet 1:12-21	
Tuesday	Amos 9:1-15	2 Pet 2:1-8	
Wednesday	Hos 1:1-9; 3:1-5	2 Pet 2:9-22	
Thursday	Hos 2:2-23	2 Pet 3:1-10	
Friday	Hos 4:1-10; 5:1-7	2 Pet 3:11-18	
Saturday	Hos 5:15b-7:2	Jude 1-25	
Sunday	Hos 8:1-13	Esther 1:1-3, 9-16, 19;	**Week XXIV**
		2:5-10, 16-17	
Monday	Hos 9:1-14	Esther 3:1-11	
Tuesday	Hos 10:1-15	Esther 4:1-16	
Wednesday	Hos 11:1-11	Esther 14:1-19	
Thursday	Hos 13:1-16	Esther 5:1-14; 7:1-10	
Friday	Hos 14:1-9	Baruch 1:14-2:5; 3:1-8	
Saturday	2 Kgs 15:1-5, 32-		
	35; 16:1-8	Baruch 3:9-15, 24-4:4	
Sunday	Is 6:1-13	Tobit 1:1-22	**Week XXV**
Monday	Is 3:1-15	Tobit 2:1-3:6	
Tuesday	Is 5:8-13, 17-24	Tobit 3:7-17	
Wednesday	Is 7:1-17	Tobit 4:1-5, 19-21; 5:1-16	
Thursday	Is 9:8-10:4	Tobit 6:1-17	
Friday	Is 28:1-6, 14-22	Tobit 7:1, 8b-17; 8:5-13	
Saturday	Mic 1:1-9; 2:1-11	Tobit 10:7c-11:15	
Sunday	Mic 3:1-12	Judith 2:1-6; 3:6; 4:1-2,	**Week XXVI**
		9-15	
Monday	Mic 6:1-15	Judith 5:1-21	
Tuesday	2 Kgs 17:1-18	Judith 6:1-21; 7:1,4-5	
Wednesday	2 Kgs 17:24-41	Judith 8:1a, 10-14, 28-	
		33; 9:1-14	
Thursday	1 Chr 29:1-2;	Judith 10:1-5, 11-17;	
	30:1-16a	11:1-8, 20-23	
Friday	Is 20:1-6	Judith 12:1-13:2	
Saturday	2 Kgs 20:1-19	Judith 13:3-14:7	

		Year 1	Year 2
Week XXVII	Sunday	Is 22:1-14	Sir 1:1-20
	Monday	Is 30:1-18	Sir 2:1-18
	Tuesday	2 Kgs 18:17-36	Sir 3:1-16
	Wednesday	2 Kgs 18:37-19: 19, 35-37	Sir 3:17-4:10
	Thursday	Is 37:21-35	Sir 5:1-6:4
	Friday	2 Kgs 21:1-18, 23-22:1	Sir 6:5-37
	Saturday	Zeph 1:1-7, 14-2:3	Sir 7:22-36
Week XXVIII	Sunday	Zeph 3:8-20	Sir 10:6-18
	Monday	Jer 1:1-19	Sir 11:11-28
	Tuesday	Jer 2:1-13, 20-25	Sir 14:20-15:10
	Wednesday	Jer 3:1-5, 19-4:4	Sir 15:11-20
	Thursday	Jer 4:5-8, 13-28	Sir 16:24-17:14
	Friday	Jer 7:1-20	Sir 17:15-32
	Saturday	Jer 9:2-12, 17-22	Sir 24:1-22
Week XXIX	Sunday	2 Kgs 22:8, 10-23:4, 21-23	Sir 26:1-4, 9-18
	Monday	Nahum 1:1-8; 3:1-7, 12-15a	Sir 27:22-28, 7
	Tuesday	2 Chr 35:20-36:12	Sir 29:1-13;31:1-4
	Wednesday	Hab 1:1-2:4	Sir 35:1-17
	Thursday	Hab 2:5-20	Sir 38:24-39:11
	Friday	Jer 22:10-30	Sir 42:15-25; 43:27-33
	Saturday	Jer 19:1-5, 10-20:6	Sir 51:1-12
Week XXX	Sunday	Jer 23:9-17, 21-29	Wisd 1:1-15
	Monday	Jer 25:15-17, 27-38	Wisd 1:16-2:24
	Tuesday	Jer 36:1-10, 21-32	Wisd 3:1-19
	Wednesday	Jer 24:1-10	Wisd 4:1-20
	Thursday	Jer 27:1-15	Wisd 5:1-23
	Friday	Jer 28:1-17	Wisd 6:1-25
	Saturday	Jer 29:1-14	Wisd 7:15-30
Week XXXI	Sunday	2 Kgs 24:20b-25:13, 18-21	Wisd 8:1-21
	Monday	Jer 37:21; 38: 14-28	Wisd 9:1-18
	Tuesday	Jer 32:6-10, 26-40	Wisd 10:1-11:4
	Wednesday	Jer 30:18-31:9	Wisd 11:20b-12:2, 11b-19
	Thursday	Jer 31:15-22, 27-34	Wisd 13:1-10; 14:15-21; 15:1-6
	Friday	Jer 42:1-16; 43:4-7	Wisd 15:18-16:13, 20-25
	Saturday	Ezek 1:3-14, 22-2:28	Wisd 18:1-15a; 19:4-9

	Year 1	Year 2	
Sunday	Ezek 2:8-3:11, 16-21	1 Macc 1:1-24	**Week XXXII**
Monday	Ezek 5:1-17	1 Macc 1:41-64	
Tuesday	Ezek 8:1-6a, 16-9:11	2 Macc 6:12-31	
Wednesday	Ezek 10:18-22; 11:14-25	2 Macc 7:1-19	
Thursday	Ezek 12:1-16	2 Macc 7:20-41	
Friday	Ezek 13:1-16	1 Macc 2:1, 15-28, 42-50, 65-70	
Saturday	Ezek 14:12-23	1 Macc 3:1-26	
Sunday	Ezek 16:3-19, 35-43, 59-63	1 Macc 4:36-59	**Week XXXIII**
Monday	Ezek 17:3-15, 19-24	2 Macc 12:36-45	
Tuesday	Ezek 18:1-13, 20-32	1 Macc 6:1-17	
Wednesday	Ezek 20:27-44	1 Macc 9:1-22	
Thursday	Ezek 24:15-27	Dan 1:1-21	
Friday	Ezek 28:1-19	Dan 2:1, 25-47	
Saturday	Ezek 34:1-6, 11-16, 25-31	Dan 3:8-23, 24-30	
Sunday	Solemnity of Christ the King Dan 7:1-27		**Week XXXIV**
Monday	Ezek 36:16-36	Dan 5:1-17, 23-31	
Tuesday	Ezek 37:1-14	Dan 6:4-27	
Wednesday	Ezek 37:15-28	Dan 8:1-26	
Thursday	Ezek 38:14-39:10	Dan 9:1-4, 18-27	
Friday	Ezek 40:1-4; 43:1-12; 44:6-9	Dan 10:1-21	
Saturday	Ezek 47:1-12	Dan 12:1-13	

Index

Hymns

Psalms

Canticles

Other